MW00951866

A Six-Week Curriculum for Kids

THOMAS NELSON
Since 1798

NASHVILLE DALLAS MEXICO CITY RIO DE JANEIRO BEIJING

Compiled by Dorla Schlitt.

Published by Thomas Nelson, Inc., P.O. Box 141000, Nashville, Tennessee, 37214.

Unless otherwise indicated, all Scripture quotations are from The Holy Bible: New Century Version (NCV). Copyright © 1987, 1988, 1991 by W Publishing Group, a Division of Thomas Nelson, Inc. Used by permission. All rights reserved.

Library of Congress Cataloging-in-Publication Data is available.

Printed in the United States of America.
  3 4 5 VG 08 07

Contents

✓

Introduction

Teachers,

*As you read through the lessons included in **Splash!**, I hope you will be as excited as your children to visit the W–E–L–L each day!*

Let the Bible stories come alive as you teach and share about the living God who knows and loves each of your children, who provides for them, and invites them to continually come to him for eternal life and eternal refreshment.

All of the various activities in this curriculum are designed to draw children in, and to help them develop a real thirst for Jesus. Included is an assortment of enrichment activities, all of which have been designed to serve your age group.

May you and your children enjoy drinking from the well of life, together!

Be Blessed,

Thomas Nelson, Inc.

Splash!

Lesson 1

The Woman at the Well

Background

Jacob's well can still be visited today. It is located in the center of the town, Sychar, in Samaria. Approximately 9 ft. wide and well over 100 ft. deep, it is fed by a running stream that lies deep below the earth.

In Bible times the well was the only source of clean fresh water the community had for drinking and sustaining life. Each day the women of the community traveled together to the well for their water supply. Pulling, lifting, and carrying jugs of water was hard work and consumed a good amount of time. Then, due to thirst and the necessity of water for life, the women would return to the well again the next day and the next and the next.

Devotional: *John 4:1–42*

Because the Jews and Samaritans were not friends and because the Samaritan woman was a social outcast, she went alone at a different time of the day for her water. On this day the woman met Jesus at the well. Jesus met her where she was, not only in the physical but also in the spiritual. Despite all the social and political obstacles meant to prevent such a meeting, Jesus pursues her in conversation. Despite her natural inclination to avoid the truth, Jesus gently but intentionally brought her to an awareness of herself and who he is. In that moment she "drank" the living water he offered and it gushed up within her producing a woman transformed!

Aren't you and I like this Samaritan woman? By God's grace we meet Jesus at the well where we come to drink from his Word and be refreshed by his Spirit. He's there waiting for us each day. He's there to reveal himself to us and to transform our lives. As we accept his Work, rely on his Energy, trust his Lordship, and receive his Love, our thirst is satisfied. Come to the well and drink!

FOCUS

Scripture reference:
The Woman at the Well

Lesson Focus:
We are thirsty. We need to go to the well and drink.

Bible Memory:
. . . Jesus said, "Let anyone who is thirsty come to me and drink."
—John 7:37 NCV

Welcome Time (15–20 Min.)

Preparation

Construct a "well" for your classroom.

Supplies

a large appliance box approximately 3–4 ft. tall, hot glue gun/Scotch® tape, brown wrapping paper, black chalk, a 5' thin rope, a bucket, clear fixative spray, a plastic pitcher, and a sharp knife

Remove one side of the large appliance box so that the top is open. Cover the four sides with brown wrapping paper. Use hot glue or Scotch® tape to secure. Use the black chalk to draw large stones on all four sides of the box. Gently rub your hand over the chalk lines to smudge the chalk. Spray all four sides with clear fixative. Center and cut a hole at the top of one side of the box. Loop one rope end through the hole and tie a knot. Tie the bucket handle to the other rope end and lower it into the "well."

Activity

As the children come into the classroom, direct them to the center of the room where the "well" is placed. Let the children look it over, touch it, and begin to question what it is and what it is doing in their classroom. Answer their questions at this time by saying "I wonder" and repeating their question.

Transition

Sit by the well and begin to sing:
   (tune: *The Farmer in the Dell*)

     Come and sit by me.
     Come and sit by me.
     We are almost ready.
     Come and sit by me.

We're ready to begin.
We're ready to begin.
All our hands are in our laps
We're ready to begin!
Yea!

Bible Time (15–20 Min.)

"Come To the Well" Activity

Say: I wonder **what** this is? (Point to the "well" behind you.)
         Does anyone have an idea? (It's a pretend "well.")
         I wonder **what** a well is used for? (to get water)
         I wonder **why** they need to get their water from a well?
         (In Bible times there were no sinks and faucets. The well was the only place
          they could get clean fresh water.)
         I wonder **who** uses a well? (In Bible times the women would come to the well
         each day to get water for drinking.)
         I wonder **where** the water comes from? (an underground stream)
         I wonder **when** people come to the well? (when they are thirsty)
         I wonder **how** it works? (Show the children how the bucket is lowered into the
         well to fill with water and then pulled up again with the rope. Explain that the
         water is poured into the container the person brought with them. Let the
         children take turns "drawing" pretend water from the well and filling the pitcher.)

Hermie & Wormie Visit

Say: "Oh, my goodness, boys and girls, I think I hear Hermie, the caterpillar. Let's sit
         right here by the well. I do hear moaning and it's coming from over there."
         (Move to the counter and pick up the decorated "home" of Hermie and Wormie.
         Open the box, take out the puppets, and situate them properly as you speak.) It
         is Hermie! And, he has his friend, Wormie, with him.

Hermie: "Oh, boys and girls, I feel so bad! Oh my tummy hurts . . . oh . . . "

Wormie: "What's the matter, Hermie?"

3

Hermie: "Oh, my tummy hurts so bad! I was out walking this morning. It was so hot! My little legs couldn't get me home fast enough! Oh my! I was so thirsty! I looked in the fridge and tried everything I could to quench my thirst! Nothing worked! Now I'm still thirsty and my tummy hurts from all the junkie stuff I drank."

Wormie: "Sounds to me like you are dehydrated."

Hermie: "De—what?"

Wormie: "Dehydrated. That means your body needs water. Did you drink any water?"

Hermie: "No, I didn't think of water. I went straight for my favorite soft drinks."

Wormie: "No wonder you feel terrible, Hermie! Your body needs good fresh water. You need a good long drink."

Hermie: "OK. I'll be right back." (Hermie leaves Wormie and then returns.) "Gosh, Wormie, I feel better already!"

Wormie: "I'm glad, Hermie. You need to keep drinking water so you don't get dehydrated again. Right, boys and girls?"

Say: Boys and girls, Hermie learned an important lesson today. He learned the importance of listening to his body. **The next time he gets thirsty, what do you think he will do?** (Get a drink of water.)
When you get thirsty for a drink of water what do you do? (Go to the water faucet and turn on the water.)
People in Bible times couldn't do that. **Do you remember how they got a drink of water to quench their thirst?** (Go to the well.)
This morning our Bible story is about being thirsty. Let's pray before I read God's Word to you.

Prayer

Dear God, thank You for this time together. We know what it's like to be thirsty for a drink of water on a hot summer day. As we listen to your words from the Bible help us understand a different kind of thirst . . . our need for you. In Jesus' name, we pray. Amen.

Bible Story

Say: Our story takes place on a hot day. Jesus is walking with his followers from Judea to Galilee. It is a long, difficult journey. When Jesus and his followers come to the town of Sychar they stop to rest.

John 4:6–15 NCV

(Read slowly with lots of expression.
Keep eye contact with the children.)

Jacob's well was there. Jesus was tired from his long trip, so he sat down beside the well. It was about twelve o'clock noon. When a Samaritan woman came to the well to get some water, Jesus said to her, "Please give me a drink." (This happened while Jesus' followers were in town buying some food.)

The woman said, "I am surprised that you ask me for a drink, since you are a Jewish man and I am a Samaritan woman." (Jewish people are not friends with Samaritans.)

Jesus said, "If you only knew the free gift of God and who it is that is asking you for water, you would have asked him, and he would have given you living water."

The woman said, "Sir, where will you get this living water? The well is very deep, and you have nothing to get water with . . . "

Jesus answered, "Everyone who drinks this water will be thirsty again, but whoever drinks the water I give will never be thirsty. The water I give will become a spring of water gushing up inside that person, giving eternal life."

The woman said to him, "Sir, give me this water so I will never be thirsty again and will not have to come back here to get more water."

Response to the Story

(Display the poster picture of Jesus and the Samaritan woman at the well.)

Say: In our story Jesus met a Samaritan woman at the well and talked to her. **Why did she come to the well?** (To get water to drink. Her body was thirsty.) Jesus also offered her "living water." **Is "living water" different from the water that was in the well?** (yes)

"Living water" is different. The water from the well quenches our body's thirst. "Living water" quenches our thirst for God. **Did the woman want the "living water" that Jesus offered her?** (yes)

Just like the woman who comes to the well each day for her water, we need to come to God. We can ask God to teach us more about who he is. He will give us a drink from <u>his</u> well of "living water."

Display the teacher visual with the picture of the well and the letters "w . . . e . . . l . . . l."
Point to each letter as you say:

> He will teach us about his <u>work</u> on the cross, the <u>energy</u> of his Spirit, his <u>lordship</u>, and his <u>love</u>.

Bible Verse

Open your Bible again and read the verse.

Say: Today our Bible memory verse is John 7:37:
Jesus said, *"Let anyone who is thirsty come to me and drink"* (NCV).
Repeat the words after me. (Repeat the verse in phrases.)
Who can say the Bible verse by themselves?

Action Song

"Come to the Well"
(tune: *Are You Sleeping?*)

Say: OK, boys and girls, let's sing loud and clear.

We are thirsty (2x)	(Place both hands at the front of the neck.)
Yes, we are (2x)	(Shake your head "yes.")
We are thirsty	
To get a drink of water	(Raise right hand and act as if drinking water.)
Come to the well. (2x)	(Exaggerated pretend "walk" to the well.)

Dip, down, deep. (2x)	(Act as if dipping deep into the well.)
Into the well (2x)	
The water is flowing (2x)	(Move the hands in a wave motion.)
It gives us life. (2x)	(Move both hands up from in front of chest and out to each side.)

Drink, drink, gulp! (2x)	(Raise right hand and act as if drinking and gulping.)
Down it goes (2x)	(Move hand from chin to tummy.)
Deep into my body	(Put both hands on tummy.)
The water flows within me	(Move hands in wave motion.)
To quench my thirst. (2x)	(Right hand pinched fingers move away from mouth.)

Are you thirsty? (2x)	(Point out with pointer finger.)
To know God? (2x)	(Point up with pointer finger.)
God will fill you	(Put both hands on your heart.)
You'll thirst no more	(Use right hand to "pour.")
With his Holy Spirit (2x)	(Shake your head "no.")

Say: Let's sing it again and this time you try to sing along with me as we do the actions together.

Sharing Time (20–30 Min.)

Craft

Supplies:

Play-Doh®, 1/2 sheet construction paper squares, 2 craft sticks/child, Jesus figure and woman figure/child, crayons, glue

Preparation:

Small children may need to have the figures cut out for them before class time.

Activity:

<u>Make a well.</u> Show the children how to roll the Play-Doh® into a ball. Use the fingers to push out a hole in the center. Use the hands to form the sides of the well. Place the well on a 1/2 sheet of paper. Print the child's name on the paper.

<u>Make stick puppets.</u> Give each child 2 craft sticks and a figure of Jesus and a figure of the Samaritan woman. Ask the children to color the figures. When they are finished, help them glue each figure to a craft stick.

<u>Tell the story.</u> While children are finishing their craft, let those who have already finished use their puppets in retelling the Bible story to each other.

Snack Time

Tell the children not to begin eating until everyone has been served and you pray together. Ask a child to pray. If your children are young, ask them to repeat a phrase at a time as you pray. When the snack is finished, ask the older children to wipe their table area with their napkin and throw away their own leftover items. For younger children, bring the wastebasket to each one at their seat so they can help clean up.

Activity Page

Supplies:

activity pages, crayons

Activity:

Give each child an activity page. Hold a page up for them to see as you speak to the group of children.

Say: Boys and girls, please put a finger on the words at the top of the paper. This is our Bible memory verse. **Who remembers what it says?** That's right! John 7:37. " . . . Jesus . . . said . . . 'Let anyone who is thirsty come to me and drink.'"

Put your finger on "Jacob's well." **What is in the well?** (water)
Put your finger on "Jesus." **What kind of water did Jesus offer?** (living water)
Put your finger on "the Samaritan woman." **Who can tell me why she came to the well?** (to get water)
What did she receive from Jesus? (living water which is eternal life)
Put your finger on the letters at the bottom of your paper. Put your finger on the first letter. It is a "w." Use a crayon to trace over the "w." Put your finger on the second letter. It is an "e." Use a crayon to trace over the "e." Place your finger on the third letter. It is an "l." Use a crayon to trace over the "l."
Place your finger on the fourth and final letter of the word. It is also an "l" Use a crayon to trace over the "l." You have now spelled the word "well"! You may now color the picture.

Say "Good-Bye" Time (5 Min.)

At the end of your classroom time, gather your children around you and close your time together. Let them know how happy you are each one came. Recount some of the special things they did today. Remind them of how special they are to Jesus and how much he loves them.

Sing

God Is So Good

Pray

Thank you, God, for all we learned today about Your love for us. Help each of us to remember that we can come to You anytime and ask You for a drink of "living water." We do want to know You. In Jesus' name, we pray. Amen.

Enrichment Activities

Snack

Supplies:

raisins, grapes, banana slices, dehydrated banana chips, water, paper cups, napkins

Activity:

Pass out a small amount of each item on each child's napkin. Give each child a small cup of water.

Say: Let's see everyone point to their raisins. Now point to the grapes. **Did you know raisins are grapes without water?** Raisins are "dehydrated" grapes. Say "de-hy-drated." (repeat) That's a big word! Dehydrated means they are dried. When the water is removed they wrinkle up. **How do they feel?** (hard) Feel your grapes. They feel squishy. They have water inside them. Everyone point to your banana slices. Now point to a banana chip. Feel each one. **Which one is dehydrated?** (banana chip)
How did you know it was dehydrated? (It was hard.)
What is the big word that means something is without water? (dehydrated)
That's right! Good for you! Let's eat!

Which One Would YOU Drink?

Supplies:

1 small clear plastic tub with clean water, 1 small clear plastic tub with dirty water, small paper cups, 1 ladle

Activity:

Say: Look at the water in the tubs. **If you were thirsty, which one would you like to drink from? Why this one?** (It's clean.)
Why not that one? (It looks dirty.)
Are you thirsty? Would you like a drink? (Give children a drink of water.)

Application:

Say: When you are thirsty you know your body needs a drink of good clean water to quench your thirst. **Did you know there is a different kind of water and a different kind of thirst?** Today our Bible story will teach us about being "thirsty" to know God and about the special kind of water God will give us to quench our thirst.

HEY! It's Dry and Parched Here!

Supplies:

plastic container of hard, cracked soil, small pitcher of water

Activity:

Let the children "poke" the soil.

Say: **How does it feel?** (hard)
Let one child pour a small amount of water on the soil.

Say: Watch the water. **Can you see it?** (no)
Where did it go? (down into the soil)
Let the children "poke" the soil again.

Say: **How does it feel?** (still hard)
Let another child pour a little more water on the soil.

Say: Watch the water. **Can you see it now?** (no)
Where did it go? (deep down into the soil)
Let the children "poke" the soil.

Say: **How does it feel?** (softer)
Let another child pour a good amount of water on the soil.

Say: Watch the water. **Can you see it now?** (no)
Where is it going? (deep, deep down into the soil)
Let the children "poke" the soil.

Say: **How does it feel now?** (soft)

Application:

Say: This soil was hard and cracked because it was so dry. **What did it need?**
(water)
When you poured water on the soil where did the water go?
(deep down into the soil)
Can we see where the water went? (no)
Now when you feel the soil it feels soft. We can tell from the feel of the soil that the water changed the soil from hard to soft. **Did you know that deep inside of everyone is a special place no one can see with their eyes?** The Bible

calls it our "heart." It's not the heart that goes "thump, thump." Our "heart" is like this soil. When we act mean and cranky, our "heart" is telling us it is thirsty.

Measuring Jacob's Well

Supplies:

masking tape, lots of rulers

Preparation:

Prior to class measure a 9' diameter circle in your classroom or hallway. Mark it with masking tape. Measure 100' of masking tape down the hallway. If your hallway is not that long measure an increment of 100' that you can use to illustrate how deep Jacob's well really was. (Example: Measuring 25' = 4 lengths)

Activity:

Say: **I wonder how big Jacob's well really was?** In one of the books I was reading they said the well was 9' across and over 100' deep! **Would you like to see how big that is?**

Pass out the rulers to the children. If you don't have enough tell them we will share so each person gets a chance to measure. Direct the children to the diameter of the well. Show them how to lay their rulers side by side across the middle. Help the children count the number of rulers. Direct the children to the masking tape line. Tell them the line represents the depth or how deep the well is. Show them how to lay their rulers in place and count the number of feet of tape. If the tape is not 100 feet explain how to "picture" the depth of the well. (25' = The well's depth would be 4 of these lines of tape one after another!)

Drama

Supplies:

a boy's/man's robe, a girl's/woman's robe, a woman's headscarf/towel, a plastic water pitcher, the "well"

Activity:

Talk with your children and help them understand the elements of a drama skit:

Setting:

(Where does the story take place?) The well

Characters:

(Who is in the story?) Jesus and the Samaritan woman

Props:

(What do we need?) A water pitcher the Samaritan woman brings to the well to fill with water.

Script lines:

(What do the people say?) Help the children determine the necessary conversation between Jesus and the Samaritan woman. Let the children take turns being the characters and acting out their parts.

Bible Memory Verse Game

Supplies:

small bean bag or rubber ball

Activity:

Sit on the rug in a circle with your children. Tell the children that you will say the memory verse. Then you will toss the bean bag/ball to someone in the circle. That person will say the memory verse and toss the ball to someone else in the circle, continuing until everyone has a chance to recite the Bible memory verse. If someone has difficulty saying the verse give them help.

Songs:

These are titles of additional songs that reinforce the lesson.

Deep and Wide

Deep and wide (2x)	(hands measure deep)
	(hands measure wide)
There's a fountain flowing	(wiggle fingers left to right)
deep and wide	(hands measure deep, wide)
Deep and wide (2x)	(hands measure deep, wide)
There's a fountain flowing	
deep and wide	(wiggle fingers left to right)

Try repeating the song leaving out "deep" but do the action. Repeat again leaving out "deep" and "wide" but do the actions. Finally repeat the song leaving out "deep," "wide," and "fountain" but do the actions. Try singing the song faster and faster.

Banner Over Me Is Love

I'm his child and he's my Father, and his banner over me is love. (3x)
His banner . . . over me . . . is love.
I've been drinking from the living fountain, and his banner over me is love (3x)
His banner . . . over me . . . is love.

Down in My Heart

I have the joy, joy, joy, joy down in my heart, (where?)
Down in my heart, (where?) down in my heart,
I have the joy, joy, joy, joy down in my heart (where?)
Down in my heart to stay.

Chorus:
And I'm so happy
So very happy
I have the love of Jesus in my heart.
And I'm so happy
So very happy
I have the love of Jesus in my heart.

Verse 2:
I have the love of Jesus, love of Jesus, down in my heart, (where?)
Down in my heart, (where?) down in my heart,
I have the love of Jesus, love of Jesus, down in my heart, (where?)
Down in my heart to stay.

Artwork needed for Lesson 1

For the teacher:

Picture of Jesus and Samaritan woman at the well (same as children's activity sheet pg. 17)

Drawing of Hermie & Wormie for teacher to copy on construction paper and attach to craft sticks

For the children:

Activity Page:

Top: Jesus said, *"Let anyone who is thirsty come to me and drink."* —John 7:37 NCV
Center: Drawing of Jesus, Samaritan woman, and well
Bottom: Letters for tracing W e l l

Supply list for Lesson 1

Welcoming Activity

3'–4' tall appliance box
hot glue/Scotch® tape
brown wrapping paper
black chalk
5' thin rope
bucket
clear spray fixative
plastic pitcher
sharp knife

Bible Time

Bible
shoe box
green & brown construction paper
2 craft sticks
Hermie & Wormie copy sheet
Drawing of Jesus & Samaritan woman at the well
Song lyrics: *"Come to the Well"*
Sharing Time
Play-Doh®
construction paper
craft sticks
Jesus & Samaritan woman story figures
crayons
glue

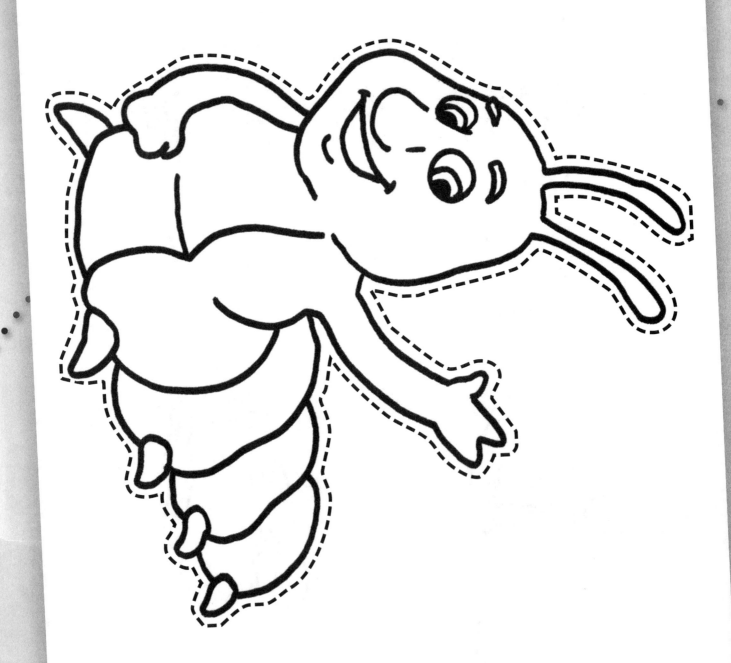

19

NOTES NOTES NOTES NOTES

Splash!

Lesson 2

The Story of Lazarus

Background: *John 11:1–45*

After reading the Bible story of Lazarus reread verses 35 and 43. Do you see both the humanity and divinity of Christ? Now consider these facts. The story of Lazarus happens less than a month before Jesus' own death and resurrection. The town of Bethany where Lazarus and his sisters, Mary and Martha, lived was less than 2 miles from where Jesus and his disciples were. Bethany was only a one-day journey. In Bible times beliefs concerning death were as varied as they are today. Jewish people believed the soul stayed near the body for three days after death. Finally, Jesus called Mary, Martha, and Lazarus "friends." They had a relationship with him and he loved them.

Devotional

Why call attention to these specific facts when there is so much to glean from the story of Lazarus? Although the facts seem unrelated, they aren't. They illustrate the wisdom, power, and goodness of God in the grace he extends to us. God's purpose and timing of the events in the lives of believers as well as in the world are always determined by his will.

We know that God's plan and purposes were established before the foundation of the earth. Jesus, the Son of God and the Son of Man, knew the purpose for which he had come into the world. He knew the purpose of coming in the flesh. He knew the purpose of each event leading to the cross. He knew the importance of God's timing and he knew the time was short. The agony of the cross and death was near. He also knew the glorious truth of the resurrection! This is God's work for us.

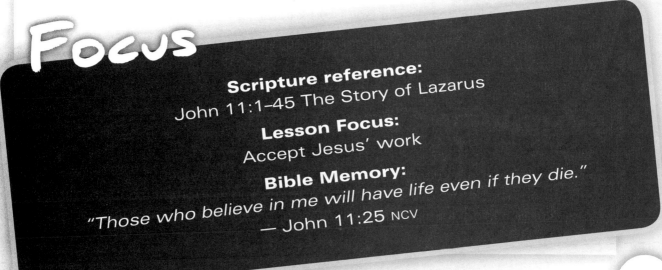

Focus

Scripture reference:
John 11:1–45 The Story of Lazarus

Lesson Focus:
Accept Jesus' work

Bible Memory:
"Those who believe in me will have life even if they die."
— John 11:25 NCV

God's timing always has a purpose. In this story the glory of God is revealed and the Son of God is glorified. If Jesus had come before Lazarus' death as Mary and Martha had asked of him, they would have only witnessed a healing. If he had come just after his death, their religious beliefs would have prevented them from believing the truth. Jesus' arrival on the 4th day was for a purpose. They were convinced by now Lazarus was dead because his body had already started to rapidly decay. He could not be resuscitated. Now they believed the only resurrection he would experience would be on the Last Day. Much to their surprise, but according to God's purpose, they witnessed a miracle that plainly showed them Jesus was the Christ, the Son of God.

There is something more we can learn in this story about God's timing. As friends of Jesus, Mary and Martha knew and trusted him. They had been hopeful and expectant of him responding in a way they were familiar. Now, as time passed, they felt disappointed and probably some anger toward their friend. More importantly their unbelief and doubt surfaced.

It was the 4th day. Mary and Martha were probably thinking, Jesus could have come sooner. He was less than two miles away! Yet, he didn't come. Had he come, this would not have happened! He knew we loved him and trusted him. He had now disappointed us in something so important to us. How could he not have intervened?

Aren't we like that? So many times we pray and pray asking God to intervene in our lives at a particular time. We wait expectantly only to be disappointed and, yes, angry. Sometimes the wait is long and very difficult to endure emotionally. Jesus knows our pain and sorrow. He wept at Lazarus' grave. He didn't weep for his friend's death. Jesus knew he would resurrect him. He wept for the pain and suffering of a fallen world.

Our friend, Jesus, will never abandon us. He is always near. His response will come even though it may not be when or as we expect. We have to trust him and know that his response will be for our good and for God's glory! Through the struggles and the blessings our thirst grows for him, for his forgiveness, for his comfort, and for his grace. This is God's work in us. Come. Drink freely from the well of grace and accept Jesus' work for you!

Welcome Time (15–20 Min.)

Preparation
Prepare a large "gift" for your children

Supplies
The largest box you can find that has a lid, a shoebox with a lid, a smaller box with a lid that fits inside the shoe box, wrapping paper, one large bow, one sheet of cardstock any color, a small wooden cross or a cross made out of 2 popsicle sticks, and a small picture of a dove

Wrap each box and lid separately. Put a large bow on the lid of the largest box. On the outside lid of the smallest box, glue the picture of the dove. On the outside lid of the shoebox, glue the wooden cross. Put the smallest box in the shoebox. Put the shoebox in the largest box. Put the lid on the box. On the cardstock "gift tag" print:

To: Those I love, I give "grace"
From: God

Tape the gift tag to the outside box. Place the large "gift" box in the center of the rug or table.

Activity
As the children come into the classroom, direct them to the "gift" box. Let the children look it over, touch it, and begin to question. What is it? What's inside it? Who's it for? Answer their questions at this time by saying "I wonder" and repeating their question.

Transition
Before you go to the area where you begin the lesson place the gift box beside the well. Prepare the Hermie and Wormie puppets by wrapping a strip of cloth around Hermie's head. Gently tape a small Dixie cup to his front as if he is holding

it. Put Hermie and Wormie behind your back where you can easily bring them out at the appropriate time.

Sit by the well with the gift box behind you. Begin to sing.
(tune: *The Farmer in the Dell*)
>Come and sit by me.
>Come and sit by me.
>We are almost ready.
>Come and sit by me.
>
>We're ready to begin.
>We're ready to begin.
>All our hands are in our laps.
>We're ready to begin!
>Yea!

Bible Time (15–20 Min.)

"Come To the Well" Activity

Say: Raise your hand if you remember what this is. (Point to the well.)
    What is it? (well)
    Do you remember what a well is used for? (To get water to drink.)
    When do people come to the well? (When they are thirsty for water.)
    Last time we were together we talked about a different kind of "thirst." We can "thirst" to know God. Just like the people in Bible times came to the well to drink, we come to God to receive his "living water." Let's do that right now. Let's pray and ask God to teach us from his word.

Prayer

    Dear God, thank you for this time together. We are thirsty to know you. We come to you. Thank you that you will give us "living water" to drink. Help us listen and understand today as you teach us from your Word, the Bible. Help us learn about your work for us and in us. In Jesus' name, we pray. Amen.

Bible Story:

Say: Our Bible story today will help us learn about Jesus and the work he did for us and wants to do in us. This story takes place in the town of Bethany where three of Jesus' friends live. They are Lazarus and his sisters, Mary and Martha.

John 11:1–45 NCV

*(Read slowly with lots of expression.
Keep eye contact with the children.)*

A man named Lazarus was sick. He lived in the town of Bethany, where his sisters, Mary and Martha also lived. Mary and Martha sent someone to tell Jesus, "Lord, the one you love is sick."

When Jesus heard this, he said, "This sickness will not end in death. It is for the glory of God." Jesus loved Martha and her sister and Lazarus. But when he heard that Lazarus was sick, he stayed where he was for two more days. Then Jesus said to his followers, "Let's go back to Judea . . . "

When Jesus arrived, he learned that Lazarus had already been dead and in the tomb for four days.

When Martha heard that Jesus was coming, she went out to meet him . . . Martha said to Jesus, "Lord, if you had been here, my brother would not have died. But I know that even now God will give you anything you ask."

Jesus said, "Your brother will rise and live again."

Martha answered, "I know that he will rise and live again in the resurrection on the last day."

Jesus said to her, "I am the resurrection and the life. Those who believe in me will have life even if they die. And anyone who lives and believes in me will never die. Martha, do you believe this?"

Martha answered, "Yes, Lord. I believe that you are the Christ, the Son of God, the One coming to the world."

After Martha said this, she went back and talked to her sister Mary alone. Martha said, "The Teacher is here and he is asking for you." When Mary heard this, she got up quickly and went to Jesus. Jesus had not yet come into the town but was still at the place where Martha had met him. The Jews were with Mary in the house, comforting her. When they saw her stand and leave quickly, they followed her, thinking she was going to the tomb to cry there.

But Mary went to the place where Jesus was. When she saw him, she fell at his feet and said, "Lord, if you had been there, my brother would not have died."

When Jesus saw Mary crying and the Jews who came with her also crying, he was upset and was deeply troubled. He asked, "Where did you bury him?"

"Come and see, Lord," they said.

Jesus cried.

So the Jews said, "See how much he loved him."

. . . Jesus came to the tomb. It was a cave with a large stone covering the entrance. Jesus said, "Move the stone away."

Martha said, "But, Lord, it has been four days since he died. There will be a bad smell."

Then Jesus said to her, "Didn't I tell you that if you believed you would see the glory of God?"

So they moved the stone away from the entrance. Then Jesus looked up and said, "Father, I thank you that you heard me. I know that you always hear me, but I said these things because of the people here around me. I want them to believe that you sent me." After Jesus said this, he cried out in a loud voice, "Lazarus, come out!" The dead man came out, his hands and feet wrapped with pieces of cloth, and a cloth around his face.

Jesus said to them, "Take the cloth off of him and let him go."

Many of the people, who had come to visit Mary and saw what Jesus did, believed in him.

Response to the Story

(Display the picture of Jesus, Mary, Martha, and Lazarus at the tomb.)

Say: In our Bible story there was a man who was sick and died.

What was his name? (Lazarus)

That's right. He had been dead and in the tomb for 4 days. His sisters, Mary and Martha, were very sad. They wanted Jesus to come while he was alive and heal him of his sickness. Jesus put off coming for a purpose. He was going to do an even greater miracle than healing Lazarus. Jesus raised Lazarus from the dead! Only God can do that! Only God has power over life and death.

Boys and girls, could Lazarus make himself come alive again? (no)

Why not? (Only God can give life.)

Did Lazarus do anything to deserve to be brought to life? (no)

When God gives us something we don't deserve it is called "grace." "Grace" is a free gift from God. We cannot earn it.

Soon after this story happened Jesus died on the cross. His death on the cross was unlike anyone else's death. Jesus took the punishment of sin for all mankind. He suffered God's anger for us. Now we can be forgiven of our sin . . . our disobedience

Something else very special happened after Jesus was buried. On the 3rd day he rose from the dead to eternal life! This means that Jesus is alive forever in heaven! Jesus' death, burial, and rising from the dead was the work God sent Jesus to do for us so we can have eternal life, too. Eternal life is a gift to us. Jesus gives it to us when we believe he died for our sin. We are just like

Lazarus. We don't deserve to be raised from the dead and we can't give ourselves life. This is grace.

Bible Verse

Open your Bible again and read the verse.

Say: Today our Bible verse is John 11:25:
            Jesus said . . . *"Those who believe in me will have life even if they die."*
            Repeat the verse after me. (Repeat the verse in phrases.)
            Who can say the Bible verse by themselves?

Hermie & Wormie Visit

Say: Oh, my, boys and girls, I think I hear Hermie and Wormie.

Hermie: (huffing and puffing) "I made it! I was hurrying my little legs off to get here in time. I'm really hot from running but I have my water with me today."

Wormie: (bring around from your back) "Hi, boys and girls! (looking over the group) "Have you seen Hermie? He was really running to get here until he ran into this big wall. (the gift box) He tried and tried to climb over it . . . but he just couldn't make it. He kept sliding back down. When I finally caught up to him, I suggested we just go around the wall. What do you know? It worked!"

Hermie: "Wormie, I'm over here! I needed a little refreshment after my long run. What was that thing we ran into?"

Say: "Do you suppose it was this?" (Point to the gift.)

Hermie: "I don't know. Let me see. (Peaks around your shoulder to see the gift.) Yikes! That thing is huge!"

Say: "You are right. I'll move this big gift so we can all see it. (Hand off the puppets and move the gift box to the center of the circle or table.) What is it? (Take the puppets in hand again.)"

Wormie: "Let me see. Up here the gift tag reads, 'To: Those I love, I give Grace. From: God'"

Hermie: "What is 'grace'?"
Say: "Grace is what God gives us that we don't deserve."

Hermie: "Like this big gift? It's not my birthday or Christmas or anything special."

Say: "Sort of like that, Hermie. Let's open the box."

Wormie: "Yes, lets do it!"

(Let a child lift the lid of the big box and bring out the shoebox with the cross on the top.)

Hermie: "It's a cross! Do we deserve the cross?"

Say: "Yes, we do. We deserve death. Even though we try really hard to obey God, we don't all the time. Do we? Have you ever disobeyed your Mommy?"

Hermie: "Yes, I have. I know that when I disobey it is sin. I need to ask God to forgive me."

Say: "That's right, Hermie, and God will forgive you because of the work Jesus did. Jesus died on the cross so you can be forgiven. Then, he rose from the dead so you can have eternal life. Someday all of God's children will rise from the dead. Let's open the next box."

(Let a child lift the lid of the shoebox and bring out the smallest box with the picture of the dove on the top.)

Hermie: "That looks like a bird!"

Wormie: "That's a dove, Hermie. A dove is gentle like the Holy Spirit. The Holy Spirit is another gift from God."

Say: "Yes, Wormie. The Holy Spirit is God's gift to every believer. He lives in our hearts. The Holy Spirit helps us know God more and more. He also helps us know when we disobey God and sin. When you disobeyed your Mommy, Hermie, and knew inside you needed to ask God's forgiveness, that's God's work in you."

Hermie: "Gosh, God's gift of grace is really big. Not only did Jesus die for us so we could be forgiven but he also gives his Holy Spirit to live in us and help us every day. I know I disobey God. I am so happy I can still know him. I do, so much, want to know him more. Don't you, boys and girls? I guess you could say I am thirsty for God. Can we sing that fun song about being thirsty for God?"

Say: "Sure. Let's stand up." (Hand off each puppet to a child to hold as they sing.)

Action Song

"Come to the Well"
(tune: *Are You Sleeping?*)

Say: OK, boys and girls, let's sing loud and clear.

We are thirsty (2x)	(Place both hands at the front of the neck.)
Yes, we are (2x)	(Shake your head "yes.")
We are thirsty	
To get a drink of water	(Raise right hand and act as if drinking water.)
Come to the well. (2x)	(Exaggerated pretend "walk" to the well.)
Dip, down, deep. (2x)	(Act as if dipping deep into the well.)
Into the well (2x)	
The water is flowing (2x)	(Move the hands in a wave motion.)
It gives us life. (2x)	(Move both hands up from in front of chest and out to each side.)
Drink, drink, gulp! (2x)	(Raise right hand and act as if drinking and gulping.)
Down it goes (2x)	(Move hand from chin to tummy.)
Deep into my body	(Put both hands on tummy.)
The water flows within me	(Move hands in wave motion.)
To quench my thirst. (2x)	(Right hand pinched fingers move away from mouth.)
Are you thirsty? (2x)	(Point out with pointer finger.)
To know God? (2x)	(Point up with pointer finger.)
God will fill you	(Put both hands on your heart.)
You'll thirst no more	(Use right hand to "pour.")
With his Holy Spirit (2x)	(Shake your head "no.")

Sharing Time (20–30 Min.)

Craft

Supplies:

red construction paper, scissors, brown strips of construction paper, paper picture of dove

Preparation:

Small children may need the red construction paper folded and cut for them and the paper figure of dove cut out for them. Prepare a sample to show the children.

Activity:

My Heart Is Meant to Be Christ's Home

Say: Before we begin our craft project I want to read a scripture to you from my Bible. " . . . *it is Christ (his Spirit) who lives in me. I still live in my body, but I live by faith (trust) in the Son of God who loved me and gave himself to save (for) me.*" —Gal. 2:20 NCV

We are going to make a picture using this Scripture. Fold the construction paper sheet in half. Fold each end of the construction paper sheet into the middle fold line.

(The teacher and any other adults in the classroom need to draw the heart for each child. Let the children do the cutting if they are able to do it accurately.) Here's my heart. (Hold up the heart made from folded paper.) Take your brown strips of paper and glue them to make a cross. Here's the cross that shows that Jesus died for me. I glued this cross to the outside door of my heart. (Show where the cross is glued.) Glue your cross to your heart. Inside my heart I will glue the picture of the little dove. (Open the "doors" of the heart to reveal the picture of the little dove.) Glue your dove to the inside of your heart.

We know that Jesus lives in heaven. It is the Holy Spirit who lives in the heart of each believer. (As the children do their project, walk to each one and ask simple questions. Let them tell you about their finished heart.)

Snack Time

Tell the children not to begin eating until everyone has been served and you pray together. Ask a child to pray. If your children are young, ask them to repeat a phrase at a time as you pray. When the snack is finished, ask the older children to wipe their table area with their napkin and throw away their own leftover items. For younger children, bring the wastebasket to each one at their seat so they can help clean up.

Activity Page

Supplies:

activity pages, crayons

Activity:

Give each child an activity page. Hold a page up for them to see as you speak to the group of children.

Say: Boys and girls, please put your finger on the words at the top of the paper. This is our Bible memory verse. **Who remembers what it says?** That's right! John 11:25. "Those who believe in me will have life even if they die."

Put your finger on the drawing of the man who is covered with a cloth. This man was in our Bible story today. **What is his name?** (Lazarus)
What can you tell me about this man? (Acknowledge right answers. Gently correct wrong answers.)
Raise your hand if you can remember the names of Lazarus' sisters. (Mary and Martha)
Put your finger on the drawing of Jesus. **What was it that Jesus did for his friend, Lazarus?** (Jesus raised Lazarus from the dead.)
Can other men do what Jesus did? (no)
Why not? (Only God can raise the dead.)
Jesus is the Son of God. Those who believe in him will have life even if they die!

Put your finger on the letters at the bottom of your paper. Put your finger on the first letter. It is a "w." Use a crayon to trace over the "w." Put your finger on the second letter. It is an "o." Use a crayon to trace over the "o." Put your finger on the third letter. It is an "r." Use a crayon to trace over the "r." Put your finger on the last letter. It is a "k." Use a crayon to trace over the "k." You have now

spelled the word "work"! Jesus came to give his life for us and then sent his Spirit to live in us. This is Christ Jesus' work.

Say "Good-Bye" Time (5 Min.)

At the end of your classroom time, gather your children around you and close your time together. Let them know how happy you are each one came. Recount some of the special things they did today. Remind them of how special they are to Jesus and how much he loves them.

Sing

God Is So Good

Pray

Thank you, God, for all we learned today. We are so thankful for your grace that freely gives us what we don't deserve. Thank you for Jesus and the work he did for us. Thank you for your Holy Spirit and the work he does in us. We are thirsty to know you, God. Quench our thirst. In Jesus' name, we pray. Amen.

Enrichment Activities

DRAMA

Supplies:

2 robes for boys, 2 robes for girls, a roll of paper towels to wrap Lazarus, a beach towel to lay on, a playground ball to roll (opt.)

Activity:

Talk with your children and help them understand the elements of a drama skit.

Setting:

(Where does the story take place?) A tomb in Bethany

Characters:

(Who is in the story?) Lazarus, Jesus, Mary, Martha (optional: townspeople, followers of Jesus)

Props:

(What do we need?) roll of paper towels, beach towel

Script lines:

(What do people say?) Help the children determine the necessary words that each character speaks. Let the children take turns being the characters and acting out their parts.

BIBLE MEMORY VERSE SONG

Optional Supplies:

musical instrument (bells/shakers/sticks)

Activity:

Pass out the musical instruments. Instruct the children to follow you around the room, singing and playing their instruments. If you don't have instruments, instruct the children to follow you around the room and clap as they sing.

(tune: *London Bridge*)

Those who believe in me
Will have life
Even if they die.
Those who believe in me
Will have life!
—John 11:25

Songs

These are titles of additional songs that reinforce the lesson.

Wonderful, Wonderful

Wonderful, wonderful, Jesus is to me.
Counselor, Prince of Peace
Mighty God is he.
Saving me, keeping me,
From all sin and shame
Wonderful is my redeemer,
Praise his name!

He'll Be Coming

(tune: *She'll Be Coming 'Round the Mountain*)

He'll be coming in clouds of glory when he comes—yee ha! (2x)
He'll be coming in clouds of glory. (2x)
He'll be coming in clouds of glory when he comes.

We will rise up to meet him when he comes—yee ha! (2x)
We will rise up to meet him. (2x)
We will rise up to meet him when he comes.

"LITTLE SPROUT" ACTIVITY

Supplies:

lima beans, water, napkins, tooth picks, zip lock plastic bag, paper towels

Preparation:

Soak a lima bean in water overnight for each child. Transport the soft beans to class in a covered container with the beans protected by layers of wet paper towels. Transport the hard lima beans in a zip lock plastic bag.

Activity:

Lay a napkin in front of each child. Lay a soft lima bean and a hard lima bean on each napkin. Let the children gently touch the lima beans.

Say: Touch each lima bean. How do they feel? (One feels soft. The other feels hard.) These lima beans are like two different hearts. The hard bean is like the heart that doesn't know Jesus. The soft bean was soaked in water. Water softened it. The water is like the Holy Spirit. The Holy Spirit softens our heart so we can believe and know God. Those who believe in Jesus receive life. Even though their bodies die, they will live in heaven in new bodies.
Take the toothpick. Gently open the soft bean. The soft outer shell falls away just like our bodies do when we die. Look what is inside. Do you see the new little sprout? This little sprout is alive and will live and grow into what Jesus made it to be . . . a bean plant. Someday each one of us will die. But, if we trust Jesus, he will give us a new life in heaven.

When believers die we are sad. We will miss them. We need to remember that someday we will see them again in heaven. They are living in heaven with Jesus!

WOODWORKING ACTIVITY

Supplies:

scrap pieces of wood, hammer, nails

Activity:

Allow the children to hammer the nails into the wood to make a cross. When a child finishes building his cross ask these questions:

What did you build? (a cross)
Who died on a cross? (Jesus)
Why did Jesus die on the cross? (to take my punishment for disobeying God)
When they buried Jesus, did he stay in the tomb? (no)
What happened to Jesus? (God raised him from the dead.)
Will you have to die for your sin? (no)
Why not? (Jesus died for me. If I believe in him I can receive eternal life.)
Why did you make the cross? (To remind me of what Jesus did for me.)

"FRIEND" GAME

Supplies:

paper, pencils, timer, chalkboard/white board, chalk/erasable marker, eraser, candy for everyone

Preparation:

Make a list of words or phrases that describe "being friends."

Activity:

Divide the class into as many small groups as you have adult helpers in the room. Give each adult a group of children. Give each adult paper and pencil. Explain to the class that when you give the signal to start, the adult will quickly record their team's responses to this direction: Name as many words or phrases that you can think of in 3 minutes that describe the relationship of being "friends." Turn the timer to 3 minutes and say "go." At the end of 3 minutes say "Stop. Put your pencils down."

Say: **What group has a list of 10 or more descriptive words or phrases?**
(If no one has that many, drop to 8.)
Please read off your list and I'll record them. (List their responses on the chalkboard/white board.)
Does any other group have something different to add to the list? (Record additions.)

Lazarus, Mary, Martha, and Jesus were friends. Jesus wants to be our "friend," too. He wants to have a relationship with each of you. These are some of the characteristics of a friendship. Close your eyes for a minute and listen to me as I read the list. Think about whether these words describe your relationship with Jesus. Then we'll pray.

Pray:
Dear God, thank you for Jesus. Thank you that he wants us to know him as "friend." Please help each one of us to know him in that way. We know he loves us. Teach us what it means to love him. In Jesus' name, we pray. Amen.

"LIVING" OR "NOT LIVING" ACTIVITY

Supplies:
a collection of items that exemplify living and nonliving (a rock, a book, a plant, a bug in a jar, a butterfly in a jar, a goldfish, a pencil, a leaf, a flower in a container of water)

Activity:
Display the items on the table. As the children look over the items, ask them this question: **What do you see on the table that is living or has life? What things do you see that are not living?** Things that are living take in food and get energy from the food so they can move. They grow, adapt to where they live, and make more of the same thing. Goldfish make more goldfish. **Who is it that gives these things "life"?** (God) **When the flower, or the bug, or the goldfish dies, can we make it come back to life?** (no) **Why not?** (Only God has the power to give life.)

Artwork needed for Lesson 2

For the teacher:
Crafts sheet (pg. 40)

For the children:
Activity sheet (pg. 42)

Supply list for Lesson 2

Welcoming Activity
Large box with lid
Shoe box with lid
Small box with lid

Large bow
Wrapping paper
1 sheet cardstock
small wooden cross or 2 craft sticks
small picture of dove
hot glue/glue
marker
Scotch® tape

Bible Time

Bible
Hermie & Wormie puppets
Small Dixie cup
Small strip of cloth
Song lyrics: *"Come to the Well"*
Drawing of Lazarus, Mary, Martha, Jesus at tomb

Sharing Time

Red construction paper
Scissors
Brown construction paper strips
glue
picture of dove
crayons
Activity sheet

Open like doors

Fold · Fold

Jesus said, "Those who believe in me will have life even if they die." John 11:25

work

NOTES NOTES NOTES NOTES

Splash!

44

Lesson 3

The Holy Spirit

Background: *John 7:37–39a The Holy Spirit*

From before the foundation of the earth the Holy Spirit has moved in perfect unity with God and his Word. How do we learn about this mysterious member of the godhead? God instructs us through his Word, especially in the Book of John in the New Testament. Although invisible to our eyes, the Holy Spirit's presence is very real. He lives in the heart of every believer. His purpose there is to transform the heart of the believer into the image or character likeness of Christ. The Bible tells us it is not by our own ability or power that this can be done. Our hearts are changed only by the power of the Holy Spirit.

Devotional

Think for a moment about the presence of the Holy Spirit in your own life. The moment you first believed the gospel, did you know God's Holy Spirit came into your heart and became a new creation in Christ? (2 Cor. 5:17) At that time you probably didn't know much about the Holy Spirit. You knew God had saved you and someday you would go to heaven. Now what?

As you began to learn from God's Word about the Holy Spirit's personhood and his work, how did you respond? Were you fearful? Curious? Open to all that God had for you? Do you still thirst for God? Or have you slipped into indifference? Do you really want the Holy Spirit to transform you into the character and likeness of Christ? If so, ask, wait, and pray. By the power of the Holy Spirit, Christ will be formed in you. Pray for his Spirit to energize and work in you. Pray for God's love to flow out from you to others like a "river of living water." Oh, Holy Spirit,

Focus

Scripture reference:
John 7:37–39a The Holy Spirit

Lesson Focus:
Rely on His Energy: The Holy Spirit

Bible Memory:
"You will not succeed by your own strength or power, but by my Spirit," says the LORD All-Powerful.
—Zech. 4:6

give us a deep thirst to be like Jesus. Draw us to the well of life and give us "living water." Help us to drink and drink and drink.

Welcome Time (15–20 Min.)

Preparation

Prepare several "glove" puppets for your children

Supplies

Depending on the size of your class provide enough yellow heavy latex gloves that children can easily share, fine tip markers in various colors.

Use a fine tip marker to draw a big happy face on the palm of each glove. Use the fine tip colored markers to draw these very simple pictures on the palm side of each fingertip. Do all the gloves alike.

Thumb: Draw a round circle with a big smile.
Pointer finger: Draw a round circle with two eyes.
Middle finger: Draw a round circle with stick legs and feet at the bottom of the circle.
Ring finger: Draw a round circle with ears on each side.
Pinkie finger: Draw a round circle with two stick arms and 5 fingers coming out from each side.

Place all of the gloves on the table in your classroom.

Activity

As the children come into the classroom, direct them to the table with the gloves. Let the children try them on, interact with one another, and ask questions. What are these? What are they for? Who gets to use them? Answer their questions at this time by saying "I wonder" and repeating the question.

Transition

Supplies:

   1 yellow latex glove with pictures, yarn/ribbon, scissors, Hermie and Wormie puppets, small wooden cross & dove (Lesson 2)

Preparation:

   Prepare the Hermie and Wormie puppets. You will need the little wooden cross and the small drawing of the dove. Gently tape the little wooden cross to Hermie and the little dove to Wormie. Cut 5 short lengths of ribbon/yarn and tie a bow at the bottom of each finger of the yellow latex glove.

   Sit by the well with the glove in your lap. Lay Hermie and Wormie behind you. Begin to sing.

   (tune: *The Farmer in the Dell*)
   Come and sit by me.
   Come and sit by me
   We are almost ready.
   Come and sit by me.

   We're ready to begin.
   We're ready to begin.
   All our hands are in our laps.
   We're ready to begin!
   Yeah!

Bible Time (15–20 Min.)

Hermie & Wormie Visit

   (Bring Hermie and then Wormie around from your back.)

Hermie: "Gosh, did we interrupt you?"

Say: "No, Hermie. We were just beginning our Sunday school lesson."

Wormie: "See, Hermie. I told you we should wait. Now we're in trouble."

Say: "No, Wormie. You aren't in trouble. We're glad to have you with us. Aren't we, boys and girls? What do you have there?"

Hermie: "We wanted to be helpers today. We each brought something from last week's lesson. Do you think the boys and girls will remember what we talked about?"

Say: "I don't know, Hermie. Let's find out. Ask them."

Hermie: "Boys and girls, I have a cross. I wonder if anyone can tell me about this cross? Who died on it and why? (Jesus. He died on the cross so we wouldn't have to. Now we can be forgiven and be a child of God.) That's right. This is the work Jesus did for us. Jesus had no sin but took our sin upon himself and gave his life for us."

Wormie: "Boys and girls, the dove on my front represents the Holy Spirit. How is a dove like the Holy Spirit? (He is gentle.) When we believe in Jesus, the Holy Spirit comes to live in our hearts. God sent the Holy Spirit to work in us . . . to help us obey God."

Say: "Wormie, what happens if it is sometimes really hard to obey God . . . like when I don't want to give up a toy?"

Wormie: "Oh, I know about that! That happens to me a lot! When it does, I ask God to help me do what's right. The Holy Spirit gives me power to obey."

Say: "Power! Wormie, we're going to talk about power today! Why don't you both stay and listen."
(Hand off the puppets to children to hold.)

"Come To the Well" Activity
Say: **Who remembers what a well is used for?** (to get a drink of water)
Where does the water come from? (an underground stream)
In Bible times when the men would dig a well, they would dig very deep. All of a sudden water comes gurgling and gushing up! (Use your hands to emphasize "gushing up.")
The water may even push rocks and soil out of the way so it can flow freely. Gushes and gurgles mean the water is moving with power. Let's pray.

Prayer

Dear God, thank you for this time together. When we are thirsty we go to the well for a drink of water. We are thirsty to know you. We come to you to receive. Teach us this morning about "living water." In Jesus' name, we pray. Amen.

Bible Story

Say: In the Scripture today Jesus is speaking to a crowd of people. They are in Judea for a special feast or celebration.

John 7: 37–39a NCV

(Read slowly with lots of expression.
Keep eye contact with the children.)

On the last and most important day of the feast Jesus stood up and said in a loud voice, "Let anyone who is thirsty come to me and drink. If anyone believes in me, rivers of living water will flow out from that person's heart, as the Scripture says." Jesus was talking about the Holy Spirit.

Say: **Who was Jesus talking about in this Scripture?** (The Holy Spirit)
What did Jesus say the Holy Spirit was like? (The Holy Spirit is like a "river of living water.")
How is the Holy Spirit like a river? (The Holy Spirit moves with power like a river moves with power.)

(Show the children the glove.)
Say: This glove will help us learn more about the Holy Spirit.

(Hold on to the end of the glove. Put your hand into the glove and make a fist.)
This is like your heart when you believe in Jesus. God's Spirit comes in it to live.

(Hold up each limp finger.)
The Holy Spirit wants to help you love others like Jesus would love them. We can't do that by ourselves. It's hard to love some people! **Why is it hard to love others?** (They aren't nice to us!)

How do we get his help? (Ask him.)
That's right. We can pray.

(Lay the glove down and take off the little ribbons/yarn. Push your fingers fully into the glove.)

God's Spirit wants to live BIG in you! He wants to fill your heart with his presence and his power to obey God. He also wants to flow out of your heart as love to others . . . just like a river!

(Point to each gloved finger as you speak)

The Holy Spirit will help you say kind words.
The Holy Spirit will help you walk with Jesus.
The Holy Spirit will help you see ways to love others.
The Holy Spirit will help you learn right from wrong.
The Holy Spirit will use your hands to help others.

Response to Bible Time

Say: Boys and girls, we have learned many things today about the Holy Spirit. **What are some things we learned about him? Where does the Holy Spirit live? What does he do? How do we receive the Holy Spirit's help?**

(The Holy Spirit lives in a believer's heart. The Holy Spirit is like a river of living water that flows from our heart. The Holy Spirit helps us love others even when it is hard. The Holy Spirit helps us obey God. We can pray and ask the Holy Spirit to help us. The Holy Spirit changes us to be more like Jesus.)

Bible Verse

Open your Bible again and read the verse.

Say: Today our Bible verse is Zechariah 4:6. *"'You will not succeed by your own strength or power, but by my Spirit,' says the Lord All-Powerful."*

Repeat the verse after me. (Repeat the verse in phrases.)
Who can say the Bible verse by themselves?
What does it mean?
(It means that we do not have the power to help ourselves or to change our heart. Only God's Holy Spirit has the power we need.)

(Teacher takes Hermie and Wormie in her hands.)

Hermie: Gosh, talking about loving others even when it's hard makes me know I need help. I'm not very good at being nice when someone isn't nice to me.

Say: Hermie, we all have that struggle. That's why we need Jesus. We want to obey. We thirst inside to please Jesus.

Wormie: Can we sing that special song again and pretend we are drinking God's Spirit before Hermie and I have to leave?

Say: Sure. Let's stand up.

Splash!

Action Song

"Come to the Well"
(tune: *Are You Sleeping?*)

Say: OK, boys and girls, let's sing loud and clear.

We are thirsty (2x)	(Place both hands at the front of the neck.)
Yes, we are (2x)	(Shake your head "yes.")
We are thirsty	
To get a drink of water	(Raise right hand and act as if drinking water.)
Come to the well. (2x)	(Exaggerated pretend "walk" to the well.)
Dip, down, deep. (2x)	(Act as if dipping deep into the well.)
Into the well (2x)	
The water is flowing (2x)	(Move the hands in a wave motion.)
It gives us life. (2x)	(Move both hands up from in front of chest and out to each side.)
Drink, drink, gulp! (2x)	(Raise right hand and act as if drinking and gulping.)
Down it goes (2x)	(Move hand from chin to tummy.)
Deep into my body	(Put both hands on tummy.)
The water flows within me	(Move hands in wave motion.)
To quench my thirst. (2x)	(Right hand pinched fingers move away from mouth.)
Are you thirsty? (2x)	(Point out with pointer finger.)
To know God? (2x)	(Point up with pointer finger.)
God will fill you	(Put both hands on your heart.)
You'll thirst no more	(Use right hand to "pour.")
With his Holy Spirit (2x)	(Shake your head "no.")

52

Sharing Time (20–30 Min.)

Craft

Supplies:

brown paper lunch bags, copies of boy and girl puppet faces, crayons, scissors, glue, colored yarn for hair (older children: colored construction paper scraps or fabric/felt scraps for puppet clothing)

Preparation:

Small children need the puppet faces cut out for them.

Activity:

Making puppets

Say: Today we are going to make puppets. When you slip your hand inside your puppet it is like God's Spirit inside of you. You are helping your puppet talk just like the Holy Spirit helps you say kind words and tell others about Jesus and his love.

Each child should receive a brown paper bag and a puppet face. Cut out the puppet face pieces. Glue the two pieces of the puppet face to the bottom flap of the brown paper bag. The boy or girl appears to move their mouth. Younger children use yarn and crayons to make hair and clothing. Older children may use several craft supplies to make the hair and clothing for their puppet.

Allow some time for the children to use their puppets in talking to one another or sharing what they learned in their lesson about the Holy Spirit. Ask them questions and let them use their puppet to answer.

Snack Time

Tell the children not to begin eating until everyone has been served and you pray together. Ask a child to pray. If your children are young, ask them to repeat a phrase at a time as you pray. When the snack is finished, ask the older children to

wipe their table area with their napkin and throw away their own leftover items. For younger children, bring the wastebasket to each one at their seat so they can help clean up.

Activity Page

Supplies:

activity page, crayons

Activity:

Give each child an activity page. Hold a page up for them to see as you speak to the group of children.

Say: Boys and girls, please put your finger on the words at the top of the paper. This is our Bible memory verse. Who remembers what it says? That's right!

"'You will not succeed by your own strength or power, but by my Spirit,' says the LORD All-Powerful" (Zech. 4:6).

Do you see the drawing of our glove? Find the thumb on this glove drawing. Put your finger on it. Look at the picture. **How does the Holy Spirit help us?** (We speak kind words.)
Find the pointer finger on this glove drawing. Put your finger on it. Look at the picture. **How does the Holy Spirit help us?** (We walk with Jesus.)
Find the middle finger on this glove drawing. Put your finger on it. Look at the picture. **How does the Holy Spirit help us?** (We see ways to help others.)
Find the finger with the ring on it. Put your finger on it. Look at the picture. **How does the Holy Spirit help us?** (We learn right from wrong.)
Find the pinkie finger—the littlest finger. Put your finger on it. Look at the picture. **How does the Holy Spirit help us?** (Our hands help others.)

At the bottom of the page is a word. The word is "energy." God's Spirit is very powerful. He gives his power or energy to us so we can obey God. Let's spell this word.

Put your finger on the "E." Trace it with your crayon. Put your finger on the "n." Trace it with your crayon. Put your finger on the "e." Trace it with your crayon Put your finger on the "r." Trace it with your crayon. Put your finger on the "g." Trace it with your crayon. Put your finger on the "y." Trace it with your crayon. **What does the word spell?** Energy! You may now color your glove.

Say "Good-Bye" Time (5 Min.)

At the end of your classroom time, gather your children around you and close your time together. Let them know how happy you are each one came. Recount some of the special things they did today. Remind them of how special they are to Jesus and how much he loves them.

Sing

God Is So Good

Pray

Thank you, God, for all we learned today about your Holy Spirit. Thank you that your Spirit is with us all the time to help us obey you and love others as we should. Help us remember to come to you and keep drinking of your Spirit. We do want to know you. In Jesus' name, we pray. Amen.

Enrichment Activities

DRAMA/GAME

Supplies:

a small basket or container, slips of plain paper, pencil, wrapped candy

Preparation:

Print each activity on a separate slip of paper. Put the slips in the basket.

Someone took away your favorite toy. An aunt you don't know is visiting and she walks toward you to give you a big hug and kiss. You want to swing but there is a long line waiting for turns. The puppy just knocked down your tall Lego® tower. You are on your bed reading an interesting book and mother calls you to dinner. Mom just baked a chocolate cake and you are hungry. You have just finished dinner and your favorite TV show is on. You see your mom coming up the stairs carrying

bags of groceries. You just left grandma's with a bag of gum drops. Your mom stops off at a friend's house to deliver a package. A little boy comes over to your car to see you. You have a dentist appointment and you hate going to the dentist.

Activity:

Say: Today we are going to play a game that requires a little bit of acting. We'll act out how <u>we would want</u> to respond and how the <u>Holy Spirit would want us</u> to respond.

Divide the class into 2 teams. Choose names for the teams. Have the teams sit in 2 lines facing each other on the floor or in chairs. Number the children facing each other in each team the same. The first child from each team stands. The teacher takes a slip of paper from the basket and reads the first activity.

First team #1:   Act out how you might want to respond.
Second team #1:   Act out how the Holy Spirit would help you respond . . . the right way . . . the loving way.

Continue with the activities until each person on both teams has had a chance to act out an activity. Give everyone a piece of candy for doing so well together.

BIBLE MEMORY ACTION VERSE

It's not by strength   (Punch right fist into left palm.)
It's not by power   (Clench fists and "show" muscles.)
But by my Spirit   (Hands over heart)
Says the Lord   (Point up)

SONGS

These are titles of additional songs that reinforce the lesson.

Oh, Be Careful

(tune: *If You're Happy*)

Oh, be careful little eyes what you see   (point to eyes)
Oh, be careful little eyes what you see
For the Father up above is looking down in love (point up)
So be careful little eyes what you see.

Oh, be careful little ears what you hear . . .   (cup hands around ears)
Oh, be careful little hands what you do . . .   (hold out hands)
Oh, be careful little feet where you go . . .   (point to feet)
Oh, be careful little heart whom you trust . . .   (hands over heart)

Oh, be careful little mind what you think . . .   (point to temple)

This Little Light of Mine

This little light of mine   (Hold up left forefinger.)
I'm gonna let it shine
This little light of mine
I'm gonna let it shine
Let it shine, let it shine
Let it shine.

Hide it under a bushel?   (Cover finger with right palm.)
NO!   (Shout "NO" and uncover finger.)
I'm gonna let it shine.
Hide it under a bushel? NO!
I'm gonna let it shine,
Let it shine, let it shine
Let it shine.

Don't let anybody blow it out   (Blow at top of finger instead of singing
                                    "blow.")

I'm gonna let it shine
Don't let anybody blow it out
I'm gonna let it shine
Let it shine, let it shine
Let it shine.

Jesus Loves Me

Jesus loves me, this I know
For the Bible tells me so.
Little ones to him belong
They are weak, but he is strong
Yes, Jesus loves me. (3x)
The Bible tells me so.

HEART GAME

Supplies:
    2 large sheets of red craft paper, scissors, black marker

Preparation:
    Fold the red craft paper sheets in half and cut to form two large hearts. Cut the
hearts into "puzzle" pieces. On each puzzle piece of each heart print a word that

represents an area of life the Holy Spirit wants to help children with. Do the same for the second heart.

Sharing	Patient
Helping	Loving
Kind	Joyful
Obeying	Gentle

Activity:

Talk with your children about the words on each puzzle piece and how the Holy Spirit gives us power to obey God. Divide the class into pairs. Let each pair race against each other in putting together their own big heart.

DRINK ANYONE?

Supplies:

2 small slightly wilted philodendron plants, small containers of alcohol and clean water (labeled), 2 plastic spoons

Activity:

At the beginning of class show the children the philodendron plants.

Say: **What do you suppose is wrong with these plants?**
(They need a drink of water.)
What kind of drink should we give them? We have two liquids. We have alcohol. (Point to the alcohol.) We have water. (Point to the water.) Let's do an experiment.

Allow a child to put a few spoonfuls of alcohol on one plant. Another child puts a few spoonfuls of water on the second plant. Label each plant according to the "drink" it received. Put the plants on the shelf until the end of class.

At the end of class show the two plants to your class.

Say: **Do you see a difference in the plants?** (yes)
What happened to the plant that received alcohol to "drink"? (It looks no different or it looks worse.)
What happened to the plant that received the water to "drink"?
(It has revived some.)
Why do you suppose one plant did well and the other did not? (God didn't plan for plants to "drink" alcohol. He planned for them to be revived and kept alive with water.)

Explain to your children that we are like these plants. God designed you to be filled with his Spirit . . . the Holy Spirit, God's living water. God wants you to have his life within you to give you the power, strength, and energy to live for him.

Artwork needed for Lesson 3

For the teacher:
Craft sheet of puppet faces to run copies for children (pg. 60, 61)

For the children:
Activity sheet (pg. 62)

Supply list for Lesson 3

Welcoming Activity
Yellow latex gloves
Fine tip colored markers
Yarn/ribbon
Hermie & Wormie color sheet

Bible Time
Lesson 2 supplies
small wooden cross, dove picture
Scotch® tape
Hermie & Wormie puppets
Song lyrics "Come to the Well"

Sharing Time
Brown lunch bags
Boy & girl puppet faces
Scissors
Glue
Crayons
Yarn
Colored construction paper scraps
Fabric/felt scraps
Activity sheet

"You will not succeed by your own
strength or power, but by my spirit,"
says the LORD All-Powerful.
Zechariah 4:6

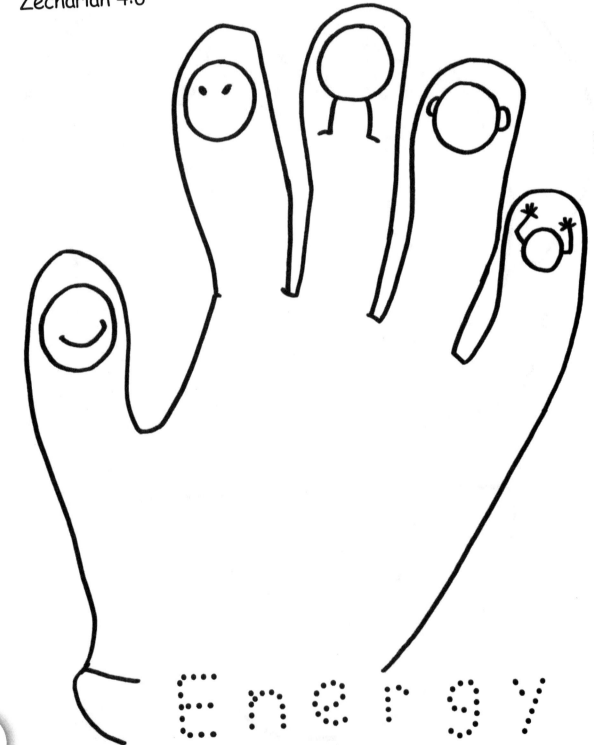

Energy

NOTES NOTES NOTES NOTES

Splash!

Lesson 4

Jesus Calms the Storm

Background: *Luke 8:22–25 Jesus Calms the Storm*

The story "Jesus Calms the Storm" takes place on the Sea of Galilee. The Sea of Galilee is a large lake that is fed by the Jordan River. Rising to the north of the sea is Mt. Hermon which is 9,200 feet tall. Because the Sea of Galilee is 690' below sea level, there are often strong and very sudden storms that blow through the gorges into this area.

On this particular day, Jesus and his disciples had gotten into a boat to go over to the other side of the lake. As Jesus was sleeping in the boat a storm arose with such intensity the waves rocked the ship and filled it with water. To the disciples' natural eyes there was a very real and present danger. After all, some of them were fisherman and knew the sea. They had probably had some experience themselves in rough waters or had heard stories of storms destroying ships and fishermen.

Though these men had seen Jesus perform many miracles in the past, they were overcome with fear and went straight to Jesus for help. As they woke Jesus from sleep they accused him of not caring. Without a word to the disciples, Jesus stood to His feet and rebuked the storm. By the power and authority of his word, the sea immediately became calm. Then, turning to the disciples, Jesus does not scold them for disturbing him, but rather asks a question that forces them to consider their own spiritual condition.

"Where is your faith?"

Focus

Scripture references:
Luke 8:22–25; Matt. 8:24–27; Mark 4:35–44 Jesus Calms the Storm

Lesson Focus:
Trust God's Lordship

Bible Memory:
"Give all your worries to him, because he cares about you."
—1 Pet. 5:7 NCV

Devotional

Where is your faith? What a question? As Christians, we know we are not exempt from the "storms of life." They seem to come out of nowhere with the ability to rock our boat. Just like the disciples, our natural eyes tend to focus on the circumstances we find ourselves in. However, there is another "storm" going on at the same time that we don't see. This "storm" rages within our own heart. With our eyes focused on our circumstances the thoughts of "what if" assail us. We move from a place of faith and trust to a place of fear and unbelief in a matter of moments. "Where is your faith?" Jesus asks each of us. Is my faith in things I hope will keep my life "tranquil?" Is my faith in my good job, my bank account, my good health? These things could change any moment. Jesus wants our hearts at peace no matter the circumstances life may give us. How can that happen? We must learn to accept God's sovereignty and lordship over our lives. Each storm we encounter and pass through is designed by God to helps us accept his lordship and receive his peace. Jesus was present in the boat with the disciples and Jesus' presence dwells within us. Jesus spoke directly to the storm and it ceased. Jesus gives us his Word to speak into our lives and heart so that his power and authority can rule over our emotions and give us peace. Our circumstances may not change but the "storm" in our heart can be arrested. Only Jesus can give that inner peace. We need that peace. We are thirsty for that peace. We need to drink from God's well of lordship.

Welcome Time (15–20 Min.)

Preparation:

Prepare several "boats in a bottle" for your children.

Supplies:

several 2 liter plastic soda bottles with lids, water, blue food color, popsicle sticks

Pour water into each bottle until it is about half full.
Put a few drops of blue food coloring into each bottle of water.
Drop a popsicle stick into each water bottle.
Tightly secure the lids to all the bottles.

Place all the water bottles on their sides on the classroom table.

Activity:

As the children come into the classroom, direct them to the table with the water bottles. Let the children pick the plastic bottles up and swish the water back and forth as they interact with one another. What are these supposed to be? Why is there a popsicle stick in there? Answer their questions at this time by saying "I wonder" and repeating their question.

Transition

Supplies:

masking tape, one of the plastic soda bottles with blue water, Hermie and Wormie puppets, globe/map of the world (opt.)

Preparation:

Near the well, use the masking tape to make an outline on the classroom floor of a boat for you and your children to sit in.

Activity:

Sit inside the "boat" with the plastic soda bottle in your lap. Lay Hermie and Wormie behind you along with the globe/map. Begin to sing.

(tune: *The Farmer in the Dell*)
Come and sit by me.
Come and sit by me.
We are almost ready.
Come and sit by me.

We're ready to begin.
We're ready to begin.
All our hands are in our laps.
We're ready to begin!
Yeah!

Splash!

Bible Time (15–20 Min.)

"Come To the Well" Activity

Say: **When you came to the table this morning you found "this."** (Hold up the plastic soda bottle with the blue water and popsicle.)
I wonder what the blue water reminds you of? (the ocean, the lake, the river, the sea)
I wonder what the popsicle stick is supposed to be? (a boat)
I wonder what happens when I gently move the bottle back and forth horizontally? (Move the bottle) (The water begins to swish and make "waves.")
Do you see the "boat"? What is happening to it? (It is bouncing up and down with the water. Sometimes it even goes underwater.)

Our Bible story today is about Jesus. He and his followers are on a boat. Jesus uses their boat ride to teach them and us a very important lesson. Before we hear that story, let's pray together.

Prayer

Dear God, thank you for this time together. We come to you this morning. We are thirsty to know you. Use this Bible story to teach us more about you. You are our God and we are your children. In Jesus' name, we pray. Amen.

Bible Story

Say: Our Bible story today takes place near the Sea of Galilee where Jesus has been teaching crowds of people about God and his kingdom. (Show the children the United States and then where the Sea of Galilee is located.)
The Sea of Galilee is like a big lake. Some of Jesus' disciples were fishermen and knew that storms with lots of wind often came up quickly on this lake.

Luke 8:22–25 NCV

*(Read slowly with lots of expression.
Keep eye contact with the children.)*

One day Jesus and his followers got into a boat, and he said to them, "Let's go across the lake." And so they started across. While they were sailing, Jesus fell asleep. A very strong wind blew up on the lake, causing the boat to fill with water, and they were in danger. The followers went to Jesus and woke him, saying, "Master! Master! We will drown!" Jesus got up and gave a command to the wind and the waves. They stopped, and it became calm. Jesus said to his followers, "Where is your faith?" The followers were afraid and amazed and said to each other, "Who is this that commands even the wind and the water, and they obey him?"

Response to Bible Time

Say: **Who was asleep in the boat when the storm began?** (Jesus)
Who was afraid? (Jesus' followers)
Why were Jesus' followers afraid? (They were in a bad storm. The boat was filling with water.)

What did the disciples do? (They went to Jesus for help.)
What did Jesus do? (Jesus told the wind and waves to stop.)

I wonder. **What do you think this story tells us about Jesus?** (He is God. He is all powerful. He can do anything.)
That's right! Jesus is King. He rules over the heavens and the earth. All things obey his command. He is Lord.

I wonder. In this story the disciples were in a storm and were afraid. **Did they remember that Jesus was with them?** (yes)
What did they do? (They went to Jesus for help.)

I wonder. **Has there been a time when you were afraid or worried? Did you remember that Jesus is always with you? What can you do when you are worried or afraid?** (You can ask God for his help anytime.)

Bible Verse

Open your Bible again and read the verse.

Say: Today our Bible verse is 1 Peter 5:7:
"Give all your worries to him, because he cares about you."

Repeat the verse after me. (Repeat the verse in phrases.)
Who can say the Bible verse by themselves? What do you think it means to "give all your worries to him"? (It means you pray and tell God your worries. You let him have them and you trust him to take care of you. You thank him for his care.)

Hermie & Wormie Visit

(Bring Hermie and Wormie around from your back.)

Hermie: Good morning boys and girls! (Say it sadly.)

Wormie: Hi everybody! (Say it peppy.) What's the matter with you, Hermie?

Hermie: Well, I'm worried. My mom said this morning that we might be moving to a different part of the garden. I don't want to move, Wormie.

Wormie: Why not?

Hermie: Well, I've never moved before. What if I don't like it? What if I have to leave you, Wormie? What if there are lots of birds who like to eat fat little caterpillars?

Say: Hermie, you know God loves you, don't you?

Hermie: Oh yes, I know that! He watches over me day and night. In fact, last week I almost got picked off a plant by this big robin. God sent a breeze just in time for me to hide under a leaf.

Wormie: Hermie, if God is taking care of you now, don't you think he will continue to do so? Even if you move to a new house?

Say: Hermie, our Bible story this morning was about trusting God even when things make us unhappy or scared. He is able to give our heart peace.

Hermie: How do I get peace and feel better inside about moving?

Wormie: You need to pray! And, you need to thank God for his care of you. He'll help you through this move to a new home. Just ask him.

Hermie: OK. Will you pray for me, Wormie?

Wormie: Sure! Dear God, You already know that Hermie's family may move to a new home. He is worried and afraid. Please give his heart peace and help him through any new changes in his life. Thank you that you care for him and love him. In Jesus' name, I pray. Amen.

Hermie: Thanks, Wormie! I'll let you know what happens. I have to go now. I have some books due at the library. Wormie, do you want to go, too?

Wormie: Sure! See you next time, boys and girls! Bye!

(Hermie & Wormie disappear behind your back.)

Say: You know, boys and girls, sometimes things happen in our lives that make us very upset. They can make us angry, or sad, or afraid, or worried. When we feel like that we are "thirsty" to know God will take care of us. When we pray, things might not change on the outside but God can give us peace on the inside. Just like Hermie. He may have to move with his family but he can know God's peace in his heart and no longer be worried about it.

Let's sing our special song and remind ourselves that Jesus is Lord over our lives. He controls all things. He is well able to help us through any difficult experience we might have in our life. Let's go to God's well of lordship and drink.

Action Song

"Come to the Well"
(tune: *Are You Sleeping?*)

Say: OK, boys and girls, let's sing loud and clear.

We are thirsty (2x)	(Place both hands at the front of the neck.)
Yes, we are (2x)	(Shake your head "yes.")
We are thirsty	
To get a drink of water	(Raise right hand and act as if drinking water.)
Come to the well. (2x)	(Exaggerated pretend "walk" to the well.)

Dip, down, deep. (2x)	(Act as if dipping deep into the well.)
Into the well (2x)	
The water is flowing (2x)	(Move the hands in a wave motion.)
It gives us life. (2x)	(Move both hands up from in front of chest and out to each side.)

Drink, drink, gulp! (2x)	(Raise right hand and act as if drinking and gulping.)
Down it goes (2x)	(Move hand from chin to tummy.)
Deep into my body	(Put both hands on tummy.)
The water flows within me	(Move hands in wave motion.)
To quench my thirst. (2x)	(Right hand pinched fingers move away from mouth.)

Are you thirsty? (2x)	(Point out with pointer finger.)
To know God? (2x)	(Point up with pointer finger.)
God will fill you	(Put both hands on your heart.)
You'll thirst no more	(Use right hand to "pour.")
With his Holy Spirit (2x)	(Shake your head "no.")

Sharing Time (20–30 Min.)

Craft

Supplies:

1/2 sheets colored construction paper, copies of Jesus and pictures of things that can worry us, glue, crayons, stapler, fine tip markers

Preparation:

For younger children, cut around each figure of Jesus, cut on the lines separating the little pictures, and fold each 1/2 sheet of construction paper to make a "book cover." On the front of the book cover, print "Jesus is Lord" at the top.

Activity:

Making little books

Say: Today we are making little books. When we read our little books we will be reminded that Jesus is Lord over all things. When we pray and give him our worries, He will give us his peace.

Each child should receive a 1/2 sheet of colored construction paper, a drawing of Jesus, a page of small drawings that may scare us or make us worry.

Fold the 1/2 sheet of construction paper in half to make a "book cover."
Print "Jesus is Lord" at the top with a fine tip marker.
Glue the picture of Jesus to the front cover.
Show the children how to cut on the lines of the small drawing sheet.
Stack the pictures together and place inside the "book cover."
Staple along the fold of the cover holding the "pages" in place.
Color each picture.

Allow time for the children to use their little books to "read" to each other. Help the children learn to say "Jesus is Lord over _____. (the storm)"

Snack Time

Tell the children not to begin eating until everyone has been served and you pray together. Ask a child to pray. If your children are young, ask them to repeat a phrase at a time as you pray. When the snack is finished, ask the older children to wipe their area with their napkin and throw away their own leftover items. For younger children, bring the wastebasket to each one at their seat so they can help clean up.

Activity Page

Supplies:

activity page, crayons

Activity:

Give each child an activity page. Hold a page up for them to see as you speak to the group of children.

Say: Boys and girls, put your finger on the words at the top of the paper. This is our Bible memory verse. **Who remembers what it says?** That's right! *"Give all your worries to him, because he cares about you"* (1 Pet. 5:7).

Find Jesus in this picture and point to him. **Remember our Bible story this morning? What do you suppose Jesus is doing in this picture?** (He is commanding the storm to stop.)
Jesus is Lord. He is in control of all things. We can trust that he will take care of us because he loves us.

At the bottom of the page is a group of words. **Do you recognize the first word?** It is "Jesus." That's right! It says "Jesus is . . . " **What is the last word?** (Lord) Let's spell it out as you trace the letters.
Put your crayon on the first letter. This is a capital "L." Trace it. Put your crayon on the second letter. This is an "o." Trace it. Put your crayon on the third letter. This is an "r." Trace it. Put your crayon on the last letter. This is a "d." Trace it. **What does the word spell?** (Lord) Jesus is Lord.
You may now color the drawing.

Say "Good-Bye" Time (5 Min.)

At the end of your classroom time, gather your children around you and close your time together. Let them know how happy you are each one came. Recount some of the special things they did today. Remind them of how special they are to Jesus and how much he loves them.

Sing

God Is So Good

Pray

Thank you, God, for all we learned today about your lordship over all things and over us. Thank you that you are with us all the time to care for us. Help us remember to come to you when we are afraid or worried. You will give us your peace and help us through difficult times. We can trust you, Lord Jesus. In your name, we pray. Amen.

Enrichment Activities

SNACK

Supplies:

angel food cake, Cool Whip®, spoons, small plastic cups

Preparation:

Cut up an angel food cake into bite size pieces. Layer cake and Cool Whip® in small plastic cups.

Activity:

Angel Food Snack Treat

Say: Our snack is a real treat today! Angel food cake and Cool Whip® are light and airy. They remind us of the angels who live above the clouds in heaven. The

Bible tells us that God created angels to worship him and serve him in heaven. God also sends angels to protect and watch over us. We can't see them but they are there. We can thank God for his protection.

DRAMA

Supplies:

masking tape "boat" on the floor, man's robe for "Jesus," 12" dowels/paint sticks with blue crepe paper streamers attached to the ends

Activity:

Today we are going to act out our Bible story of Jesus and his followers in the boat during the storm. We will need someone to be "Jesus," some of you to be "his followers," and some of you to be "the waves and the wind."

Explain to the children that those who are "waves and wind" will sit outside the boat and wave their "water" streamers and make wind sounds. Those who are Jesus' followers will sit inside the boat with Jesus.

Discuss those elements of a drama:
Setting
Characters
Props
Script *(Read Mark 4:38, 39, 41)*
Action

Allow the children to enact the scene over and over, getting a chance to change roles.

BIBLE MEMORY VERSE SONG

(tune: *The Farmer in the Dell*)
Give all your worries to him (3x)
Because he cares for you.
(say: 1 Peter 5:7)

BIBLE MEMORY VERSE ACTIVITY

Supplies:

1 large sheet of construction paper, yarn, hole punch, picture of Jesus, slips of blank paper, pencils, glue

Preparation:

Make a "Prayer Pouch" prior to class from folded construction paper with a yarn handle. Glue a picture or drawing of Jesus on the pouch. Hang the pouch somewhere in the classroom.

Activity

At Bible Memory Verse time show the children the Prayer Pouch. Let the children pretend to write on slips of paper anything they are worried about or afraid of. Let them take their "worry" and give it to Jesus by putting it in the Prayer Pouch. Hold the Prayer Pouch in your hands and as a class pray and thank God for taking all their worries and helping each one of them to trust God to care for them.

SONGS:

These are titles of additional songs that reinforce the lesson.

He's Got the Whole World

He's got the whole world in his hands (4x)

He's got the little, bitty baby in his hands (4x)
He's got you and me brother (4x)
He's got you and me sister (4x)
He's got everybody here (4x)
He's got the wind and the rain (4x)
He's got the sun and the moon (4x)

My God Is So Great

My God is so great, so strong and so mighty!	(Hold up arms and flex muscles.)
There's nothing my God cannot do. (clap, clap)	(Shake head "no.") (2x)
The mountains are his, the rivers are his,	(Make hands form mountain peak, wiggle fingers from left to right.)
The stars are his hand-i-work too.	(Fingers make twinkling stars.)
My God is so great, so strong and so mighty!	(Hold up arms and flex muscles.)
There's nothing my God cannot do! For you!	(Point up.)

Rise and Shine

(Divide the children into 2 groups, everybody sings.)

Rise and shine and give God the glory, glory (2x)   (1st group stands up, hands in front, palms up and lift, move upper body side to side in rhythm.)

Rise and shine and (clap) give God the glory, glory   (2nd group stands up, hands in front, palms up and lift, move upper body side to side in rhythm.)

Children of the Lord
We Bow Down
He Is Lord
I Love You, Lord

FLOAT/SINK ACTIVITY

Supplies:

a collection of common items that will float and sink, a small tub of water, paper towels

Activity:

Children can experiment with different items to see if they will float or sink.

Say: Today our Bible story involves water, a storm, and a boat. **Do boats float?** (yes) **What happens if a boat gets filled with water?** (It will sink.) **If you were in a boat and it began to fill with water would you be afraid?** (yes) (No, I can swim.) The story we are going to hear is about Jesus and his followers. They were on a boat when a very bad storm came up. I wonder what happens?

Artwork needed for Lesson 4

Activity Sheet:

verse, drawing, words "Jesus is Lord."
copy sheet of "Jesus" (pg. 80); copy sheet of small pictures (pg. 81)

Supply list for Lesson 3

Welcome Activity

2 liter plastic soda bottles with lids
water
blue food color
popsicle sticks
masking tape

Bible Time

Hermie & Wormie puppets
Song lyrics *"Come to the Well"*

Sharing Time

Construction paper
"Jesus" pictures
"Small" pictures
stapler
glue
crayons
fine tip markers
activity sheet

Give all your worries to him,
because he cares about you.
1 Peter 5:7

Jesus is Lord

NOTES NOTES NOTES NOTES

Splash!

Lesson 5

God Loves You

Background: *Luke 22:31–34, 54-62; John 21:1–17*

The Bible is full of Scriptures that speak of God's love for his people. Why is it then that the reality of God's unconditional love for us is so difficult to receive and we struggle with loving others as God loves? The answer is one word . . . sin. The heart of a sinful man has no love for God and his love for others is selfish and distorted. How can we know God's unconditional love? We go to the source—God. God is love. To know God's love we must be born of God. Romans 5:5 says that God pours his love into our heart by the Holy Spirit whom he has given us when we are born of God. According to 1 Thess. 3:12, he makes his love increase in our heart and overflow to others. His love transforms our lives. Read through the story of Peter's denial of Christ. What a story of divine grace illustrating God's unconditional love!

Devotional

Aren't we just like Peter? We listen as the Lord speaks through his word. We see the providence of his loving hand in our lives. We sense the sweet comfort of his presence in prayer. We believe we are strong in our faith until, like Peter, life has a way of suddenly showing us how weak our faith really is. Like Peter we realize how much we need God's forgiveness and restoration. As God keeps pouring his love into our hearts, that love transforms our lives. Come drink

Focus

Scripture reference:
Matt. 26:33–35; 69–75
Mark 14:27–31; 66–72
Luke 22:31–34; 54–62
John 13:37, 38; 18:15–27; 21:1–17

Lesson focus:
Receive God's Love

Bible Memory:
"We love because God first loved us."
—1 John 4:19

Splash!

from the well of God's love. Drink knowing his love for you is unconditional and everlasting. Be refreshed, renewed, and restored. Drink and keep drinking.

Welcome Time (15–20 Min.)

Preparation

"Soak-it-up" activity

Supplies

several types and sizes of hard, dry sponges, small tubs of water, plastic tablecloth/newspaper

Protect the activity area with a plastic tablecloth or newspapers. Place the tubs of water where the children can easily and safely reach them. Lay the sponges around the tubs.

Activity

As the children come into the classroom, direct them to the activity area where the tubs of water and sponges are located. Let the children experiment with putting each sponge into the water, soaking up the water, and squeezing the water out of the sponge and back into the tub. Let the children ask questions. What are these? What are they for? What are we going to do with these today? Answer their questions at this time by saying "I wonder" and repeating their question.

Transition

Supplies:

tub of water, sponge, Hermie & Wormie puppets with small wet sections of cloth draped over their heads like "towels"

Activity:

Sit by the well and begin to sing
(tune: *The Farmer in the Dell*)
> Come and sit by me.
> Come and sit by me.

We are almost ready.
Come and sit by me.

We're ready to begin.
We're ready to begin.
All our hands are in our laps.
We're ready to begin.
Yeah!

Bible Time (15–20 Min.)

"Come To the Well" Activity

Say: This morning many of you were trying out the sponges and the water. **What did you discover about the dry sponge when it was put deep into the water?** (It soaked up the water.)
Is the sponge soft or hard now? (soft)
Let's pretend the water in the tub is God's love. God's love is like an ocean! It is so big and so deep! There is no end to God's love! It's really too big for us to completely understand.

Let's pretend the dry sponge is our heart. The sponge is dry because it is thirsty for water just like our hearts are thirsty to know God's love. Just like this sponge soaks up water when I put it in the water, God wants our hearts to soak up and be filled with his love. When we realize how much God loves us, we will be able to love others so much better. (Squeeze the sponge.) His love comes pouring out of us just like the water comes pouring out of this sponge. **Is the sponge still hard and dry?** (no)
The water changed the sponge, and God's love will change our heart. **If the sponge is left out of the water what will happen?** (It will dry out.)
That's right. Our hearts can become dry, too. We become thirsty for more of God's love. We must remind ourselves often of how much God loves us. We need to take big gulps of God's love and take them often!

In fact, let's do that right now. Everybody stand up.

Action Song

"Come to the Well"
(tune: *Are You Sleeping?*)

Say: OK, boys and girls, let's sing loud and clear.

We are thirsty (2x)   (Place both hands at the front of the neck.)
Yes, we are (2x)   (Shake your head "yes.")
We are thirsty
To get a drink of water   (Raise right hand and act as if drinking water.)
Come to the well. (2x)   (Exaggerated pretend "walk" to the well.)

Dip, down, deep. (2x)   (Act as if dipping deep into the well.)
Into the well (2x)
The water is flowing (2x)   (Move the hands in a wave motion.)
It gives us life. (2x)   (Move both hands up from in front of chest and
                             out to each side.)

Drink, drink, gulp! (2x)   (Raise right hand and act as if drinking and
                             gulping.)
Down it goes (2x)   (Move hand from chin to tummy.)
Deep into my body   (Put both hands on tummy.)
The water flows within me   (Move hands in wave motion.)
To quench my thirst. (2x)   (Right hand pinched fingers move away from
                             mouth.)

Are you thirsty? (2x)   (Point out with pointer finger.)
To know God? (2x)   (Point up with pointer finger.)
God will fill you   (Put both hands on your heart.)
You'll thirst no more   (Use right hand to "pour.")
With his Holy Spirit (2x)   (Shake your head "no.")

Prayer

Dear God, thank you for this time together. Thank you that your word tells us that you showed your own love for us in this: "While we were still sinners, Christ died for us" (Rom. 5:8 NIV). We don't deserve your love. We can't earn your love. We can't even understand the great love you have for each of us. But, dear God, we can receive your love. Teach us today about your love for us and how we can accept it. In Jesus' name, we pray. Amen.

Bible Story:

Say: Our Bible story today is about Jesus' love for us. We learn about Jesus' love from a man named Peter or Simon. Peter was a fisherman until Jesus called him to be his follower. Peter loved Jesus very much. He had seen Jesus do many miracles. Jesus had taught him about God and his kingdom. Peter believed Jesus was the Christ, the Son of the living God. At the time of this story, Jesus and his followers were having their last meal together before Jesus' death. Jesus speaks.

Luke 22:31-34, 54-62;
John 21:1-17 NCV

(Read slowly with lots of expression.
Keep eye contact with the children.)

"Simon, Simon. Satan has asked to test all of you as a farmer sifts his wheat. I have prayed that you will not lose your faith! Help your brothers be stronger when you come back to me." But Peter said to Jesus, "Lord, I am ready to go with you to prison and even to die with you!" But Jesus said, "Peter, before the rooster crows this day, you will say three times that you don't know me."

They (the Roman soldiers) arrested Jesus, and led him away, and brought him into the house of the high priest. Peter followed far behind them. After the soldiers started a fire in the middle of the courtyard and sat together, Peter sat with them. A servant girl saw Peter sitting here in the firelight, and looking closely at him, she said, "This man was also with him." But Peter said this was not true; he said, "Woman, I don't know him."

A short time later another person saw Peter and said, "You are also one of them." But Peter said, "Man, I am not!" About an hour later, another man insisted, "Certainly this man was with him, because he is from Galilee, too." But Peter said, "Man, I don't know what you are talking about!" At once, while Peter was still speaking, a rooster crowed. Then the Lord turned and looked straight at Peter. And Peter remembered what the Lord had said, "Before the rooster crows this day, you will say three times that you don't know me." Then Peter went outside and cried painfully.

Response to the Story

Why did Peter cry? (He was sad. He had said he didn't know Jesus.) That's right. Peter was very sorry for what he had said and how he had acted. Raise your hand if you have ever felt really sorry for something you said to someone.

Raise your hand if you have ever felt really sorry for something you did that was wrong.

Then you know how Peter felt.

This is not the end of the story. After Jesus was raised from the dead, he showed himself to his followers three times. On one such time Peter and several others were fishing when they saw Jesus on the shore beside a fire of hot coals. Peter jumped into the water and began swimming to shore. The rest of Jesus' followers followed Peter in the boat. When they reached shore, Jesus invited them to eat some fish with him. Jesus made no mention of what Peter had said and how he had acted earlier. Jesus simply asked him three times, "Peter, do you love me?" Each time Peter responded, "Yes, Lord."

From this story we learn that Jesus loves us even when we do things or say things that aren't pleasing to him. His love is unconditional. We cannot make him love us any more or any less. Nothing can change his love for us and nothing can separate us from his love (Rom. 8:38, 39).

Hermie & Wormie Visit

Say:　　　Oh, my goodness, Hermie & Wormie! What happened to you both?

Hermie:　　Well, Wormie and I overheard you talking to the boys and girls about "soaking up God's love." We decided to go for a swim and get some of God's love, but all we got was wet!

Say:　　　Oh, Hermie, I'm so sorry! A sponge soaks up water. We soak up God's love through God's word. God's word teaches us about God's love!

Wormie:　　See, Hermie! I knew we weren't going to find God's love down at the creek!

Say:　　　That's OK. You both are thirsty to know God's love. You need to go to God not to the creek! God's love is <u>everlasting</u> and <u>unconditional</u>. That means it has always been and it will always be. He never changes. He will always love you no matter what.

Hermie:　　Even when I do something really bad?

Say: Yes, Hermie, even if you do something really bad. He will speak to your heart about whatever you said or did that was wrong so you can ask his forgiveness, but his love for you never changes. Never be afraid to go to God when you do something wrong or need his help. He wants you to come to him.

Wormie: Hermie, remember the story of Peter when he said he didn't know Jesus? Peter was very sorry for what he had said and done. Jesus could have been very angry with Peter but he wasn't. Jesus loved Peter. Nothing could separate Peter from Jesus' love. Peter came to know God's love through that very painful experience. As a result, Peter loved God very much, and he began to tell others about God's love.

Oh, my, Hermie, look at the time. I think we'd better go. It's late.

Hermie: OK! Bye, boys and girls!

Bible Verse

Open your Bible again and read the verse

Say: Today our Bible memory verse is 1 John 4:19:
"We love because God first loved us" (NCV).
Repeat the verse after me.
Who can say the Bible verse by themselves?
Our Bible verse reminds us of God's love. Before we even know God, he knows and loves us. He created us out of his love, and nothing can separate us from his love.

Splash!

Sharing Time (20–30 Min.)

Craft

Supplies:

Dixie cups, knife, scissors, shades of green tissue paper, white school glue, water, small shallow dishes, water color paintbrushes, newspapers, jumbo craft sticks, small red felt hearts or heart-faceted jewels or sequins from your local craft store

Preparation:

Cover the area with newspapers. Make a small slit in the bottom of each Dixie cup. Cut the shades of green tissue paper sheets into 1/2" squares. Mix white school glue and water in each small shallow dish for each group of children to share. (Teachers with younger children may want to hot glue two jumbo craft sticks to form a cross for each child.)

Activity:

God's Love

Place two jumbo craft sticks to form a cross. Glue together. Glue the red felt heart or jewel/sequin to the center of the "cross." Let dry flat. Give each child a small amount of tissue squares, a water color paintbrush, and a Dixie cup turned upside down. The children share a small shallow dish of the glue mixture. With their paintbrush the children "paint" each tissue square onto the Dixie cup with the glue mixture. Overlap the tissue squares so that the colors mix and cover the cup completely. Let dry.

Assemble:

Slide the "cross" into the slit of the decorated Dixie cup.

As the children decorate their Dixie cups, talk to them about God's love for them. Point out that the Bible says, "God shows his great love for us in this way; Christ died for us while we were still sinners" (Rom. 5:8 NCV).

Snack Time

Tell the children not to begin eating until everyone has been served and you pray together. Ask a child to pray. If your children are young, ask them to repeat one phrase at a time as you pray. When the snack is finished, ask the older children to wipe their table area with their napkin and throw away their own leftover items. For younger children bring the wastebasket to each one at their seat so they can help clean up.

Activity Page

Supplies:

activity pages, crayons

Activity:

Give each child an activity page. Hold a page up for them to see as you speak to the group of children.

Say:　　"Boys and girls, please put your finger on the words at the top of the paper. This is our Bible memory verse. **Who remembers what it says?** That's right. *"We love because God first loved us"* (1 John 4:19).

Who do you see in this drawing? (Jesus and children)
What can you tell me about this drawing? (Jesus wants us to know we can always come to him: when we are happy, sad, angry, or feeling bad. He loves us always and forever.)

Put your finger on the letters at the bottom of the paper. Put your finger on the first letter. It is an "L." Use a crayon to trace over the "L." Put your finger on the second letter. It is an "o." Use a crayon to trace over the "o." Put your finger on the third letter. It is a "v." Use a crayon to trace over the "v." Put your finger on the last letter. It is an "e." Use a crayon to trace over the "e." You have spelled the word "love"! You may now color the picture.

Say "Good-Bye" Time (5 Min.)

At the end of classroom time gather your children around you and close your time together. Let them know how happy you are each one came. Recount some of the special things they did today. Remind them of how special they are to Jesus and how much he loves them.

Sing

God Is So Good

Pray

Thank you, God, for all we learned today about your love. Thank you that you love us so much that you sent Jesus to die for our sin and that nothing can separate us from your love. Help each of us to receive your love and remember to thank you for your love. We love you. In Jesus' name, we pray. Amen.

Enrichment Activities

SNACK

Supplies:

"heart" sugar cookies, frosting, sprinkles, paper towels, plastic knives, paper cups, water, napkins

Activity:

On a paper towel let children put icing on their own cookie and decorate it. Give each child a small cup of water.

Say: **What shape is your cookie?** (heart)
A heart makes us think of love. God loves us unconditionally. **What does "unconditionally" mean?** (It means we can't earn God's love or lose it. It means God loves us no matter what. Nothing can separate us from God's love.)

BIBLE MEMORY VERSE SONG

(tune: *Are You Sleeping?*)

We love him. (2x)
Because he first loved us (2x)
We love him
Because he first loved us.
We love him.
1 John 4:19

Songs

These are titles of additional songs that reinforce the lesson.

Oh, How I Love Jesus

Oh, how I love Jesus. (3x)
Because he first loved me.

To me he is so wonderful and I love him. (3x)
Because he first loved me.

Praise Him, Praise Him

Praise him (2x)	(raise arms above head and sway body)
All ye little children	
God is love (2x)	
(Repeat)	
Love him (2x)	(cross hands over chest)
All ye little children	
God is love (2x)	
(Repeat)	
Thank him (2x)	(hands in prayer position)
All ye little children	
God is love (2x)	
(Repeat)	
Serve him (2x)	(hands out front, palms up)
All ye little children	
God is love (2x)	
(Repeat)	

I Love You, Lord
Jesus Loves the Little Children
Jesus Loves Me

"OVERFLOWING LOVE" ACTIVITY
Supplies:

dishpan, clear plastic glass, water pitcher, water

Activity:

Children can experiment with pouring water into the plastic glass until it overflows into the dishpan.

Say: Today we learned about God's love. Romans 5:5 NIV says, *"God has poured out his love into our hearts by the Holy Spirit, whom he has given us."* God's love fills our heart and spills out to others as we care for them. **How can we care for others and show God's love?**

"HOUSE OF LOVE" ACTIVITY
Supplies:

large refrigerator box, large cardboard box, construction paper, utility knife, latex paint, newspapers/plastic tarp, large paintbrushes, plastic containers, old shirts for covering clothes, pencils, markers, decorations for paper hearts, print out of Scripture verses about God's love

Preparation:

If you have younger children, limited space, or a large group of children, you may want to "paint" the cardboard house prior to class. Stand the refrigerator box on end on the newspaper or tarp. Use the utility knife to remove one of the four sides. Cut "windows" in the remaining 3 sides. Use the utility knife to cut away the large cardboard box's two sides and top and bottom. This should leave a section of the box that resembles a pitched roof. The "roof" fits on top of the refrigerator box.

Activity:

Children take turns painting the "house." Be sure to protect good clothing with old shirts. While waiting their turn, the children make construction paper hearts to decorate the "house of love." They print a "love" Scripture on each heart and decorate the heart. The finished heart is glued to the inside of the "house."

"Love" Scriptures:

John 15:9; 1 John 4:8; Jer. 31:3; 1 Cor. 13:4–8; 1 Cor. 16:14; Rom. 5:8; Rom. 5:5; Eph. 3:18; 1 Thess. 3:12; 2 Thess. 3:5; 1 John 4:7; 1 John 4:9; 1 John 4:10; 1 John 4:16; 1 John 4:19; John 15:13

Say: Today we are making a "house of love." This will be a special place in our classroom where you can go to think about God's love for you and your love for God. You might even want to go there to thank God for his love or pray for someone to know God's love. We'll decorate this special place with hearts of love. On each heart will be a Scripture about God's love.

Artwork needed for Lesson 5

For the child:
>Activity sheet (pg. 98)

Supply list for Lesson 5

Welcome Activity
>Selection of hard, dry sponges
>Small tubs of water
>Plastic tablecloth/newspapers

Bible Time
>2 small sections of cloth for puppets' "towels"
>Song lyric *"Come to the Well"*

Sharing Time
>Dixie cups
>Knife
>Scissors
>Shades of green tissue paper
>White school glue & water
>Small shallow dishes
>Water color paint brushes
>Newspaper
>Jumbo craft sticks
>Small red felt hearts/heart-faceted jewels/sequins
>Activity page
>crayons

We love because God first loved us.
1 John 4:19

Love

NOTES NOTES NOTES NOTES

Splash!

Lesson 6

Thankfulness

Background: *Ephesians 1:2, 3; Isaiah 55:1, 3; Isaiah 58:11*

"Grace and peace to you from God our Father and the Lord Jesus Christ. Praise be to the God and Father of our Lord Jesus Christ, who has blessed us in the heavenly realms with every spiritual blessing in Christ" (Ephesians 1:2, 3).

Paul tells us that we are a spiritually blessed people. How are we spiritually blessed? God in his mercy and grace has drawn us to himself by producing a thirst within our soul that cannot be quenched by any other means except through knowing God. Jesus invites us.

"Come, all you who are thirsty, come to the waters . . . come to me . . . that your soul may live" (Isaiah 55:1, 3).

Devotional

Do you often find yourself in a place of dryness spiritually? God in his goodness and love knows our need and has provided every spiritual blessing in Christ to meet it. We simply must remember to return to him as the well of life.

Spend time in God's word. Recall the spiritual blessings he has given you. Receive his provision. Thank him for the continuous flow of grace that brings refreshment to your life. Pray the prayer of the thirsty.

"Lord, I come thirsty. I come to drink, to receive. I receive your work on the cross and in your resurrection. My sins are pardoned, and my death is defeated. I receive your energy. Empowered by your Holy Spirit, I can do all

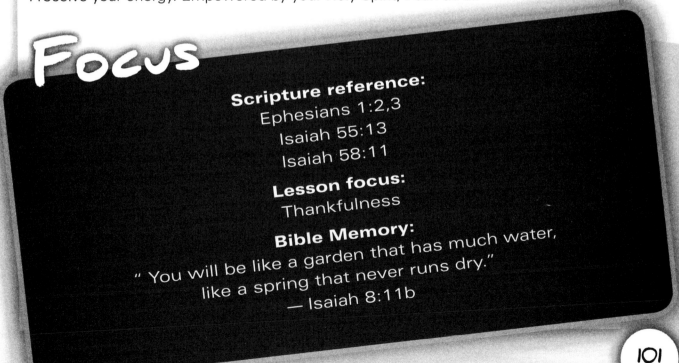

Focus

Scripture reference:
Ephesians 1:2,3
Isaiah 55:13
Isaiah 58:11

Lesson focus:
Thankfulness

Bible Memory:
" You will be like a garden that has much water, like a spring that never runs dry."
— Isaiah 8:11b

things through Christ, who gives me strength. I receive your lordship. I belong to you. Nothing comes to me that hasn't passed through you. And I receive your love. Nothing can separate me from your love."

When we continually drink from the well of life the psalmist says we "shall be like a garden that has much water, like a spring that never runs dry" (Is. 8:11b). Not only will we have life but we will bring life to others. Come and drink.

Welcome Time (15–20 Min.)

Preparation

A "Bloom'in" Activity

Supplies

large bowl of potting soil, small watering can with water, styrofoam cups for growing a flower, large spoons, colored markers, flowers to transplant, plastic tablecloth/newspapers

Protect the activity area with a plastic tablecloth or newspapers. Remove the flowers from their temporary container of soil and lay them on the table. Place the styrofoam cups for growing the flowers where the children can reach them along with the bowl of soil, the watering can, and large spoons.

Activity

Allow the children time to decorate a styrofoam cup with markers. Print their name on the cup. Oversee the children as they plant a flower in their decorated cup. Help them use the watering can to water their flower when it is planted in the soil.

As the children plant their flowers talk to them about what they are doing. Then, lead the children by example in asking "I wonder" questions. Begin with your own "I wonder" question and then ask the children. "Boys and girls, what do you wonder about this flower?" Respond by saying "I wonder that, too."

Transition

Supplies:

two exact same flowers: one flower is out of the soil with the roots showing and one flower is potted, Hermie and Wormie puppets with a silk/live flower taped to the front of each one

Activity:

Sit by the well and begin to sing (tune: The Farmer In The Dell)

Come and sit by me
Come and sit by me
We are almost ready
Come and sit by me

We're ready to begin
We're ready to begin
All our hands are in our laps
We're ready to begin.
Yeah!

Bible Time (15–20 Min.)

"Come To The Well" Activity

Say:　**I have two flowers to show you this morning.**
(Lay both the potted flower and the unpotted flower in front of the children so they can examine them.)
I wonder. How are these flowers alike?
I wonder. How are these flowers different?
I wonder. What part of this flower can't you see? (Point to the potted flower: the roots.)
I wonder. Do you know why God created flowers and plants with roots?
(Roots hold the plant in the ground. Roots draw water and nourishment from the soil. Roots store food.)

I wonder. What do you suppose will happen to this flower if it is left like this? (Point to the flower that is not potted.) It will die. It has no way of getting what it needs to live.

God is so good to provide all that a flower needs to live . . . even the little roots! The soil, the rain, and the sunlight all help the tiny flower seed grow into a beautiful flower.

Prayer

Dear God, thank you for this time together. Thank you that just as you provide for the plants in the earth you have provided for us in every way. Give us hearts that are thankful for all you have given us. In Jesus' name we pray. Amen.

Hermie And Wormie Visit

Hermie: Hey, everybody! Guess where we've been.

Wormie: Hermie, we both have a flower with us. I think the boys and girls can probably guess where we have both been.

Say: Those are very pretty flowers! Boys and girls, where do you think Hermie and Wormie have been? (to a flower garden)

Hermie: We're on our way home to put our flowers in water. You know flowers won't live long without water.

Wormie: That's right. I think we've learned a lot about water the last few weeks. I know that we need water to live, as well.

Say: That's right, Wormie. Our physical bodies get thirsty and need water to live. Our hearts get thirsty, too. To quench this thirst we must go to the Well of Life. Jesus is the Well of Life. When we come to him and receive living water the Bible says we become like a well-watered garden . . . .

Bible Verse

Hand off the puppets for children to hold. Open your Bible and read the verse.

Say: Today our Bible verse is Isaiah 58:11, "You will be like a garden that has much water, like a spring that never runs dry." Repeat the verse after me. Who can say the Bible verse by themselves?

Flowers in a garden need lots of water to live. A well-watered garden produces lots of beautiful flowers. Our lives, watered by God's Holy Spirit, are beautiful to God. They bring him glory!

Hermie: You mean I'm like a beautiful flower to God?

Wormie: I never thought of it like that. A flower's beauty is because God created it to bring him glory and he has provided all it needs to do that! It just grows and blooms!

Hermie: Gosh, God has provided all we need to grow in our faith! God has given us Jesus and the work he did at the cross. He's given us his energy . . . I mean the Holy Spirit. He provides his lordship over our lives so we can trust him to care for us. And, he gives us his love!
Wow! I just spelled the word "well": Work, Energy, Lordship, Love!

Say: You sure did! Let's stand up and sing about going to the well.

"Come to the Well"
(tune: *Are You Sleeping?*)

Say: OK, boys and girls, let's sing loud and clear.

We are thirsty (2x)	(Place both hands at the front of the neck.)
Yes, we are (2x)	(Shake your head "yes.")
We are thirsty	
To get a drink of water	(Raise right hand and act as if drinking water.)
Come to the well. (2x)	(Exaggerated pretend "walk" to the well.)
Dip, down, deep. (2x)	(Act as if dipping deep into the well.)
Into the well (2x)	
The water is flowing (2x)	(Move the hands in a wave motion.)
It gives us life. (2x)	(Move both hands up from in front of chest and out to each side.)
Drink, drink, gulp! (2x)	(Raise right hand and act as if drinking and gulping.)
Down it goes (2x)	(Move hand from chin to tummy.)
Deep into my body	(Put both hands on tummy.)
The water flows within me	(Move hands in wave motion.)
To quench my thirst. (2x)	(Right hand pinched fingers move away from mouth.)
Are you thirsty? (2x)	(Point out with pointer finger.)
To know God? (2x)	(Point up with pointer finger.)
God will fill you	(Put both hands on your heart.)
You'll thirst no more	(Use right hand to "pour.")
With his Holy Spirit (2x)	(Shake your head "no.")

Bible Story

(Hold up your Bible)

Say: **Who knows what this is?** (the Bible)

What is special about the Bible? (The Bible is God's Word.)

That's right. God gave us the Bible so that we could know him. It's like a long letter that tells us about God's great love for us and his plan to have a family of people from every nation of the world who love him, too. He has provided for all our needs and always cares for us. He is a good God. Let's spend some time today thanking God for who he is and what he has given us. Let's write a class letter together thanking him.

What would you like to say to God?

What would you like to thank him for?

Bible Response

Supplies:

Roll of white wrapping paper, masking tape, black marker, colored markers

Preparation:

Roll out the white wrapping paper and tape it to the table/wall/floor. Leave a border around the edge of the paper for the children to decorate.

Activity:

Help the children begin their letter to God.

Dear God,

We want to thank you _____.

Love,

_____

Allow the children to freely express their feelings. Record their responses on paper in sentence form. When they finish, print a closing to the letter. Show the children where to print their name at the bottom under the closing . While they wait their turn, let the children decorate the border of the letter with colored markers. Display their letter to God. Read it aloud to the children.

Sharing Time (20–30 Min.)

Craft

Supplies:

binder rings, cardstock copies of sheet with four drawings: cross, dove, crown, heart, colored markers/crayons, scissors, hole punches

Preparation:

Cut apart the pictures and punch a hole at the top of each for the younger children

Activity:

"WELL" Review

Cut apart the pictures. Punch a hole at the top of each picture. Use the colored markers/crayons to color the pictures.

As the children are coloring the pictures open each of the binder rings and help the children slip their pictures onto the ring in the appropriate order: cross (work), dove (energy), crown (lordship), and heart (love).

When the children have finished coloring talk to them about each of the pictures. Help them remember the significance of each and what it stands for: Work Energy Lordship Love

All are gifts that God gives us through Jesus Christ.

Older children might want to copy the words on the back of the appropriate picture to help them remember.

SNACK TIME

Tell the children not to begin eating until everyone has been served and you pray together. Ask a child to pray. If your children are young, ask them to repeat a phrase at a time as you pray. When the snack is finished ask the older children to wipe their table area with their napkin and throw away their own leftover items. For younger children bring the wastebasket to each one at their seat so they can help clean up.

Activity Page

Supplies:

activity page, crayons

Activity:

Give each child an activity page. Hold a page up for them to see as you speak to the group of children.

Say: "Boys and girls, please put your finger on the words at the top of the paper. This is our Bible memory verse. Who remembers what it says?

What do you see in this drawing? (flowers, a fountain)

What do you think the fountain is doing in this picture? (giving the flowers a drink of water)

The water gives the flower life. Jesus, the Fountain of Life, gives us eternal life. Though someday this body will die, we will have a new body and still be alive with Jesus in heaven.

You may now make your flower garden beautiful with lots of different colors!

Say "Good-Bye" Time (5 Min.)

At the end of your classroom time gather your children around you and close your time together. Let them know how happy you are each one came. Recount some of the special things they did today. Remind them of how special they are to Jesus and how much he loves them.

Sing

God Is So Good

Pray

Thank you, God, for all we learned today about you. Thank you that you have provided for everything we need to grow in our faith. Thank you for Jesus. Our sins are forgiven. Thank you for your Holy Spirit who helps us obey you. Thank you for your lordship in our lives and that we belong to you. And, thank you for your love and care for us. Thank you that nothing can separate us from your love. We love you. In Jesus' name we pray. Amen.

Enrichment Activities

BIBLE MEMORY VERSE SONG

(tune: Mary Had a Little Lamb)

You shall be like a watered garden
A watered garden
A watered garden
You shall be like a watered garden
Like a spring whose waters never fail.
(Is. 58:11)

BIBLE MEMORY VERSE GAME

Supplies:

music tape/CD and player, ball, wrapped soft candy

Activity:

The children sit in a circle. Begin passing the ball around the circle as the music plays. Stop the music. Whoever is holding the ball gets to say the memory verse. Help as needed. When finished give each child a piece of wrapped soft candy.

SONGS

These are titles of additional songs that reinforce the lesson.

The B-I-B-L-E

The B-I-B-L-E
Yes, that's the book for me
I stand alone
On the word of God
The B-I-B-L-E

Use construction paper and print each letter on a sheet. Choose five children to hold the papers. As you sing the song, each child holds their letter above their head. For the other lyrics they hold the letter in front of their chest.

Read, Read, Read the Word
(tune: Row, Row, Row Your Boat)

Read, read, read the Word
Before you go to bed
Merrily, merrily, merrily, merrily
Act on what is said.

Jesus, We Just Want to Thank You

Jesus, we just want to thank you (3x)
Thank you for being so good.

V2 Jesus, we just want to praise you (3x)
  Praise you for being so good.
V3 Jesus, we just want to tell you (3x)
  We love you for being so good.
V4 Jesus, we know you are coming (3x)
  Take us to live in your home.

Wonderful, Wonderful

Wonderful, wonderful,
Jesus is to me.
Counselor, Prince of Peace
Mighty God is he.
Saving me, keeping me
From all sin and shame
Wonderful is my Redeemer
Praise his name!

Hallelu, Praise Ye the Lord

Hallelu, hallelu, hallelu, hallelujah
Praise ye the Lord!
(Repeat)
Praise ye the Lord! (Hallelujah)
Praise ye the Lord! (Hallelujah)
Praise ye the Lord! (Hallelujah)
Praise ye the Lord!

Divide the class into 2 groups. One group sings the song. The second group sings "Hallelujah".

With My Hands

With my hands lifted up
And my mouth filled with praise
I will bless thee, Oh Lord (2x)
With a heart of thanksgiving, I will bless thee, Oh Lord.

"WHO REMEMBERS?"
MATCH GAME (Review Activity)

Supplies:
plastic pitcher, cross and dove, glove with finger drawings, 2 liter soda bottle with blue water, sponge, sample of each lesson's activity sheets

Preparation:
Lay the objects on the table

Activity:

Say: Today we are going to play a game that will help us remember all the different stories we have been talking about for the last few weeks. It's a match game. Here's how we will play the game.

I will hold up a picture from one of the lessons. Raise your hand if you can match the object to the story and tell us something about the story that you remember.

(If the children have difficulty remembering the lesson, give them some clues or ask them questions about the drawing. Remind them to raise their hands when they have something to share with the group. When you are finished reviewing, have the children stand up and take a bow for doing such a fine job!

"BEAN BAG TOSS" (Review Game)

Supplies:

4 different sheets of colored construction paper, black marker, beanbags, masking tape

Preparation:

On each sheet of paper draw a different symbol: cross, dove, crown, heart. Lay the symbols out on the floor. Use the masking tape and place a tape line an appropriate distance for the age of your children from the sheets of paper.

Set the children up for success. For older children you can increase the difficulty with each round depending on the interest in the game.

Activity:

Say: We are going to play a game. Each of you will get a turn to see if you can toss the beanbag onto the appropriate picture. Each picture reminds us that God has provided all we need to know him and grow in faith: the cross (Jesus' work), the dove (Holy Spirit), the crown (God's lordship), and the heart (God's love).

Everyone is to stand behind the masking tape line.
I'll give each of you a clue and you must decide which symbol I am describing. You will toss the beanbag onto that symbol. Everyone will get two tries.

Sample statements
Use your lesson materials for additional statements.

> Jesus died on this so that your sins are forgiven.
> You belong to God.
> Nothing can separate you from God's love.
> The Holy Spirit lives within the heart of every believer.
> We can receive eternal life because of Jesus' work.
> You have no reason to fear. God is always with you and cares for you.
> Because God's Spirit lives in me I can do all things with Christ's help.
> God loves you even when you disobey.

SNACK "CELEBRATION COOKIES"

Supplies:

sugar cookies, icing, decorating icing

Preparation:

Bake or purchase sugar cookies. Ice each one. Use the decorating icing to draw one of the four symbols on each cookie: cross, dove, crown, heart.

Activity:

Serve each child a cookie at snack time. As the child chooses the cookie with a symbol remind them of what it represents.

Example: "Oh, Karen, you have a crown on your cookie. The crown reminds us of God's lordship over all the earth. He is King."

Older children may be able to recall what the symbol represents.

PUPPET FUN

Supplies:

Lesson 1 copy sheet of Hermie and Wormie puppets, craft sticks, cardstock, glue

Preparation:

Run copies of Hermie and Wormie on cardstock. Cut out the figures for younger children.

Activity:

Give each child a Hermie and Wormie figure. Give each child two craft sticks. Glue the figures to a craft stick. Let dry flat.

At the close of the morning let your children divide into pairs. Each one of the pair has their own character puppet. Give them some time to pretend to talk to each other as "Hermie" and "Wormie." Ask them to tell each other about knowing God and the work Jesus did, the energy he gives us by his Holy Spirit, his lordship, and his love.

Art work needed for Lesson 6

Activity Sheet with verse and drawing of garden (pg. 117)
Sheet with four drawings: cross, dove, crown, heart (pg. 116)

Supply list for Lesson 6

Welcoming Activity

Large bowl of potting soil
Small watering can with water
Styrofoam cups
Colored markers
Large spoons
Flowers to transplant
Plastic tablecloth/newspapers

Bible Time

Hermie and Wormie puppets
Potted flower
Unspotted flower
Scotch® tape, masking tape
Two silk/real flowers for puppets
Bible
Roll of white wrapping paper
Black marker
Colored markers

Sharing Time

Binder rings
Cardstock copies of four drawings
Hole punch
Crayon/markers
Scissors
Activity pages

You will be like a garden that has much water, like a spring that never runs dry. Isaiah 58:11

Celebrate

"Goodbye!"

"See you next time!"

"Remember what we learned together!"

NOTES NOTES NOTES NOTES